# THE
# SALES
# PRO

# THE
# SALES
# PRO

**THINK** LIKE A PRO
**ACT** LIKE A PRO
**SELL** LIKE A PRO

## PAUL ANDERSON

LANGDON STREET PRESS

Published by Langdon Street Press

Cover and Interior Book Design by Monkey C Media.
www.MonkeyCMedia.com

ISBN: 978-1-63413-121-6
LCCN: 2014918488

TheSalesPro.com

*To my lifelong love, my bashert,*
*my soul mate and my inspiration,*
*all of whom are my wife:*
*Live, Love, Laura.*

*To our three children,*
*Kristina, Arabella and Calla,*
*who give meaning to the word purpose.*

# CONTENTS

# INTRODUCTION

The purpose of this book is to transform you into a sales pro as quickly as possible.

Whether you are an experienced sales person, are just graduating from college or high school, are at the beginning of a new sales position or have just been laid off from a different career, applying the professional sales and communication techniques within this book will quickly and easily allow you to close sales and achieve a level of performance equal to that of a pro—regardless of your sales cycle, the market you are selling to and the nature of your product or service.

You'll learn powerful strategies to emotionally connect to your customer and to manifest belief in what you are selling, which impacts everything you say, ensuring dynamic and powerful customer communication. Every aspect of the sales process is uncovered and every angle of the buyer's thought process is taken into account.

The interactive review exercises will enable you to customize the proven and extremely effective sales techniques of the highest-paid sales professionals, such as establishing results-based objectives for every call and using open-ended questioning to move the sale forward. The exercises will also reinforce how a sales pro focuses on the law of numbers, completes customized and dynamic winning presentations, handles customer objections so that the objection becomes the reason for buying, and creates a platform that naturally leads to closing the sale.

To become a sales pro, you must be hungry for success and excited to learn the strategies that will get you there. You will need to have complete belief in your product and a natural willingness to do whatever it takes to move a sale forward. No request should be too small. Your sense of a positive outcome with every potential customer you approach is tantamount to the success you will achieve.

## How to Use This Book

*The Sales Pro* presents the most advanced and up-to-date selling skills and strategies in their simplest form, offering anyone who is serious about becoming a professional salesperson the ability to get to the top without having to learn the hard way. My goal is for you to immediately gain from the thousands of sales calls and presentations I have made and from the knowledge I've gleaned from the hundreds of books I've read, CDs I've listened to and sales seminars I've attended.

*The Sales Pro* promotes complete comprehension of the sales techniques by dispensing insight through both text and informative cartoons. The lessons within each format are the same, but this innovative platform enables easier, faster and more effective comprehension by offering two different styles that reinforce each other to get the message across.

The main character who appears in the cartoon stories is Pete, who while attending sales school discusses with his colleagues how to apply each specific selling skill, technique and strategy. These stories will increase the rate at which you learn the particular skill and allow you to quickly apply the lesson to your own sales opportunities. The book's cartoon characters, like you, are reading about specific sales techniques; and after each major section of the book, you can follow along as they work through that chapter's lessons.

My friends and colleagues who have applied the information within this book have all achieved sales performances they hadn't thought possible. My commitment to you is if you learn and apply the selling skills and strategies in the pages to come, you too will succeed in becoming a true sales professional and earn an income you never thought possible.

Good Selling!
Paul Anderson

# ONE

# Belief: The Essential Ingredient

Selling is about building trust, and your ability to show that you are sold on what you are selling will be a fundamental principle behind your success. Fortunately I learned this at the beginning of my sales career. The first product I sold was specialized home insulation. The insulation could be blown into awkward areas of the house and was completely fireproof, and the insulation capacity was twice that of the competition, resulting in not just reduced heating bills but more consistent warmth in every room of the home. After the two-hour training session, I was convinced it was the best insulation money could buy. While most rookies went home to study the training material, I drove straight to my territory and started cold-calling door to door to make appointments so I could share this amazing information with everyone. I immediately had success in making appointments, but I knew my success would be short lived if I didn't follow through with a good presentation that reinforced the value I had been so excited to convey.

During the weeks that followed I focused on internalizing my belief in the product by increasing my knowledge of the value our existing customers were experiencing and advancing my understanding of how different the insulation was from the competition's. I reached out to the top salespeople and asked to accompany them on their calls and watched intensely as they passionately presented the information. I was amazed at how easily they interacted with their customers, what questions they would ask and were being asked and what their objectives were for each appointment. I decided to model what I was seeing and how they were acting. After the first three months the results spoke for themselves: My appointment conversion to new calls and my closing ratio to my number of appointments were soon as good as those of the most experienced salespeople.

Several months later I found myself in the position of making a dual call with another salesperson. He was lethargic and unenthusiastic, and more passionate about finishing for the night than presenting the facts about our incredible product. Needless to say, we didn't get the sale. I quickly came to realize that although we had all been given the same information as sales rookies, we were obviously not presenting it to customers in the same way. I couldn't understand why the salesperson I had presented with was even working at the company, how he had survived for so long and—though he was an average performer—why anyone would want to buy anything from him. The more I found myself in situations where I could see the other presentations salespeople were giving, the more I became aware that the majority of them showed a tremendous lack of excitement behind their words. I was constantly being asked why I was so excited about what I was saying and the product we were selling. My response was always the same: How can you not be? It was my job to show commitment for what I was saying and show absolute belief in the advantages my customer would receive through purchasing our product.

It's your job to believe with absolute certainty that what you are saying is true, honest and accurate. You don't have to believe in what you sell but you must believe in what you say. Of course, if you find yourself in the position of selling what you also believe in, your results will, without question, benefit even further.

To become a sales pro you need to manifest belief in your product by educating yourself on the story of why a potential customer should buy from you, and what makes you and the product you are selling different from your competitor and its products. What's the story behind your company's principles and values, and how can you enthusiastically present that story with conviction to inspire someone listening to emotionally connect?

You need to look behind the sales material and gain an understanding of the passion and commitment that led to the creation of the company you work for; dig even deeper to fully educate yourself on the story behind the products you are about to sell. The more you emotionally connect to the story, the more you will influence your future customers to emotionally connect, and the more powerful your presentation will be.

As you capture new sales, revisit the sales you've made and ask those customers for a testimonial that confirms they've received the benefits or financial gain you originally outlined. This will allow you to further energize your story of how good your company and its products are. Make it your story by fully committing to it with an honesty and enthusiasm that shows you really care whether your customers gain from your product's advantages. It's your job to fully own your story; if you have to, sell it to yourself over and over again and always remind yourself of the fact that there is a tremendous need for what you are offering. Sales people who cannot fully "buy in" to the product they are selling will rarely become sales pros and may be better off researching other products to sell that they can believe in.

Commit your company's major principles, values and differentiation to memory so you can recite them without thought. These points should become part of who you are, and you should be able to present them so clearly, precisely and fluently that no one questions their validity. Once you accomplish this, the enthusiasm, passion and excitement behind what you are saying will naturally flow to the customer.

Sales pros focus on visualizing their customers benefitting from their product while communicating what they believe is the best and only option available. They've naturally tapped into the law of certainty, which equals success.

It becomes obvious to your potential customer when you are talking about what you truly believe in, and you become more persuasive when he senses that you are speaking from the heart. When you become inspired, energetic and full of strong emotions, your physiology changes, your voice gets louder, your eyes sparkle and the energy you exude becomes captivating to those around you. This powerful magnetic force will set you apart.

When you are in the state of belief, people are more inclined to listen and smile as they gradually connect with your voice and its animated energy. In turn, their energy becomes inspired and they listen more intently to the details of your presentation; their defense systems close down as they fully absorb and connect with your message.

Your belief in what you say and in the value of what you are selling allows you to be authentic and honest during your presentation to your customer. Without belief, you are acting, conning or merely pretending, and it is this disconnect that separates the top sales pro from the average salesperson.

Lack of belief in your product or company dilutes your ability to respond when you receive an objection or a drawback that stops the sales process from moving forward. The non-believer is more likely to immediately accept the pushback. If you really believe that your product is the perfect solution, and you know your prospective customer will really benefit from using it, you will persist in using different techniques and approaches to ensure he is fully aware of the value. If you are giving off nonverbal vibrations of any less than 100 percent belief in what you are saying, your prospective customer will feel it.

What is it about your company or product that you really believe in? Would you buy this product tomorrow? Picture yourself at your last presentation or customer meeting. When you think back, how did you sound? How did you look? Did you honestly believe your solution was the best option? How did you feel during the meeting? Were you as enthusiastic and passionate as you are when you are thinking or talking about your family, your religion, your hometown, your country, or something as simple as the make of your car? These are beliefs that you would naturally talk about with passion, excitement and conviction, even if you are usually shy, quiet or uncomfortable speaking in public.

Sales pros treat every opportunity as though it's their last, doing whatever it takes to achieve final customer commitment. Their belief in what they are selling and the benefits their customers receive fuel their sales drive, keeping them on target without distraction until they achieve their goal. The transition to sales pro starts with the ability to emotionally connect with your product and marry the same passion you have for your personal beliefs with your passion for what you are selling.

Think about the last time you purchased something you didn't expect to buy. Why did you make the purchase? Were you told a great story, was a big need identified, or was it just a great deal? I'm sure you didn't buy from someone who was lethargic or uneducated about the benefits of her product.

Not having belief in your product or company is one of the most damaging faults of any salesperson. So why do so many salespeople not believe in their product?

1. Still learning; may lack confidence.
2. Don't feel it anymore; complacent.
3. Don't believe in the value or benefits of the product they are selling; using the company as a vehicle to get the right job.
4. Lack of training on the product, company and/or its differentiation.

Keep away from the negative, non-believing average sales performers and focus on the top salespeople, who will naturally be living, breathing and communicating their belief in what they say. Ask to spend time in the field with them to capture more insight into what they are saying, how they are saying it and what they are focusing on. Absorb their energy and watch the reaction of their clients to the specific benefits and results being presented.

There is only one limitation, and that is the one you put in your mind. You are what you believe. Whether you think you can or cannot, you're right. Whether you think your product or company is the best or the worst, you're right.

## Self-Assessment

Write down three reasons that you believe in your product/service.

1. _____

2. _____

3. _____

Write down three of your personal beliefs.

1. _____

2. _____

3. _____

Write down how the feelings of belief in your product/service compare to your personal beliefs.

_____

_____

_____

_____

# BELIEF

CARTOON STORY

# TWO

# The Power of Differentiation

Creating differentiation in your product and company is the fuel that drives your belief, and it should be the first goal of every sales person. Distinguishing what you are selling from the products or services of others is a significant key to success when you educate your potential customer on why he should give you an appointment, progress further in the sale or give you his final commitment for an order.

Your differentiation should be the core of your value proposition, which is what you propose to a potential customer to reinforce the product's value. To have a product that is designed or a company that is marketed with exclusive features enables you to focus on the benefits of those features and build value in your customer's mind as to why she should have them, thus eliminating the competition and increasing your ability to sell at a good price. This is the sales approach of every sales pro and a major reason why they succeed where the average performer fails.

In order to fully understand how to present the advantages of an exclusive feature, first identify all the features of your product or company and understand what is the function, benefit and result to your customer of each feature. This will give you direction on how to present the features correctly.

The diagram below illustrates how a sales pro emotionally connects with her customer by talking about the benefits and results she will receive from each feature, while the average sales performer tends to talk about the actual feature and its function.

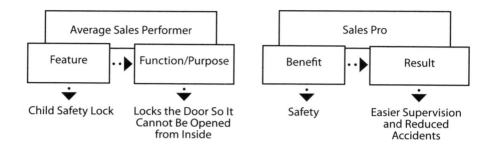

It's a common mistake of a sales rookie and, too often, the trait of average sales performers to try to sell the child safety lock (i.e., the features) and not what the product *will do* for the prospective customer (i.e., the results obtained by using it). An example of selling just a feature is a salesperson who only talks about the technical specifications of the child safety lock, while an example of selling a result of a feature is talking to a prospective customer about less worry and easier supervision.

Remember, a customer thinks in terms of the results, not the features—a person goes into a hardware shop to buy a one-inch drill because he needs a one-inch hole—so to secure the sale, you should too.

Once you have a thorough understanding of the features, function, benefits and results of each product, you'll need to develop specific questions that focus on your product's exclusive features. Begin by reviewing all the features of your product and company and compare them to those of your competition. This will immediately offer you the ability to highlight potential benefits your company offers that your competition does not.

## How to Identify Your Differentiators

The following two exercises are for the sales person who either wants to reevaluate the product and company differentiation he has been taught or to ascertain what differentiation he can establish. Once you've completed both these exercises, you will also be able to identify your competitor's differentiation, which will allow you the opportunity to strategize a counterresponse.

Exercise one identifies product differentiation and exercise two, company differentiation. Review each of your products, and based on your current knowledge and customer feedback, complete table one by incorporating your top four most commonly wanted features for each of your products. Once you have identified and listed four features, review your top three competitors. Identify their equivalent products and incorporate each of their product's corresponding features. Once this is completed, you will be able to ascertain which of your features, if any, your competition does not have. These will be your exclusive features.

| Product Differentiation Example 1 | | | | |
|---|---|---|---|---|
| | **Your Feature** | **Competitor** | **Competitor** | **Competitor** |
| Example | 240HP Engine | 180HP Engine | 160HP Engine | 185HP Engine |

Incorporate your exclusive features into table two and then complete the table with the benefit of each feature, what the result would be and if there is a financial return from the result. For example, let's say you are a salesperson selling manufacturing conveyor systems and one of the features within your conveyor is a 240HP engine that offers a processing speed 30 percent faster than your nearest competition, and the increased speed enables your customer to ship 20 percent more orders each week. If the potential customer's average order fulfillment is 100 orders a week, this exclusive feature would garner the customer an additional twenty orders per week. If the average order value is $350, these additional twenty orders would equate to $7,000 per week and an increased revenue of $364,000 per year.

| Identified Exclusive Product Feature Example 2 | | | | |
| --- | --- | --- | --- | --- |
| | **Your Feature** | **Benefit** | **Result** | **Financial Return** |
| Example | 240HP Engine | 30% increased conveyor speed | 100 more orders shipped a week | $364,000 additional annual income |

Table three should be completed if you have identified a competitor's exclusive product feature. Your advanced understanding of your competitor's differentiation will give you the time to prepare an intelligent response that could help to reduce the competitor's importance and redirect the focus back to the benefits and results of your product. For example, fingerprint security on your cell phone might sound like an excellent benefit that your competitor has but that you do not; however, what if you need someone to access your telephone when you're not with it? Perhaps you need a stored number or information from a text? Your ability to look at situations before they are in front of you increases the likelihood that you will effectively address your customer's concerns and will greatly improve your chances of moving the sale forward.

| Competitor Exclusive Product Feature Example 3 | | | | |
| --- | --- | --- | --- | --- |
| | **Competitor Exclusive Feature** | **Benefit** | **Result** | **Your Counterresponse** |
| Example | Capacitive sensor | Fingerprint security | Codes/ keyes eliminated | Reduced flexibility for approved third-party access |

## EXERCISE ONE

### Product Differentiation
### Table 1

| | Your Feature | Competitor | Competitor | Competitor |
|---|---|---|---|---|
| 1. | | | | |
| 2. | | | | |
| 3. | | | | |
| 4. | | | | |

### Identified Exclusive Product Feature
### Table 2

| | Your Feature | Benefit | Result | Financial Return |
|---|---|---|---|---|
| 1. | | | | |
| 2. | | | | |
| 3. | | | | |
| 4. | | | | |

### Competitor Exclusive Product Feature
### Table 3

| | Competitor Exclusive Feature | Benefit | Result | Your Counterresponse |
|---|---|---|---|---|
| 1. | | | | |
| 2. | | | | |
| 3. | | | | |
| 4. | | | | |

## EXERCISE TWO

### Company Differentiation
### Table 1

|  | Your Feature | Competitor | Competitor | Competitor |
|---|---|---|---|---|
| 1. |  |  |  |  |
| 2. |  |  |  |  |
| 3. |  |  |  |  |
| 4. |  |  |  |  |

### Identified Exclusive Company Benefit
### Table 2

|  | Exclusive Feature | Benefit | Result | Financial Return |
|---|---|---|---|---|
| 1. |  |  |  |  |
| 2. |  |  |  |  |
| 3. |  |  |  |  |
| 4. |  |  |  |  |

### Competitor Exclusive Company Feature
### Table 3

|  | Competitor Exclusive Feature | Benefit | Result | Your Counterresponse |
|---|---|---|---|---|
| 1. |  |  |  |  |
| 2. |  |  |  |  |
| 3. |  |  |  |  |
| 4. |  |  |  |  |

## Establishing Product and Company Criteria

Once you have established your product and company differentiation, you will be in the position of using these features to set the new criteria. It will be your job to ensure your customers understand that these specific features must be added to the criteria they have already established in order to make their buying decision. Although many potential customers may not be conscious of it, all of them will have criteria they are looking for in a new product or that they want to sustain in an existing product. Criteria simply means how they will measure or gauge what is important to them, which, once identified, will usually dictate what they will buy and who they will buy from.

Sales pros are extremely strategic with their questions. They are always looking for answers that will give them the ability to position their differentiation. They seldom make the mistake of creating desire for something that is not specifically what they can offer and that can be obtained with one of their competitors. This is why seasoned pros not only ensure they establish and meet the criteria the customer is looking for, but also make it their job to set new criteria.

The following conversation highlights a sales pro who has an exclusive product feature. Through his questions, the sales pro has determined this feature would be a major advantage to his customer. The exclusive feature is a chip within the user's smartphone that offers the user the ability to make and receive a telephone call in any country.

SALES PRO:     "Mr. Smith, what are the criteria you are looking for in a new mobile phone?"

CUSTOMER:     "Well, I want a long battery life and the ability to access the Internet while talking on the telephone and to use the telephone when I am on business trips overseas."

SALES PRO:     "Mr. Smith, this mobile phone offers you a twelve-hour battery life, which is 20 percent more than any other mobile phone, and you can access the Internet while making a call. Regarding your overseas trips, I understand you visit many countries. How do you currently handle your overseas telephone communications?"

| | |
|---|---|
| CUSTOMER: | "Well, I have to take my current phone into the store and have a special chip put in that allows me to use it. There's a different chip depending on the country I am visiting." |
| SALES PRO: | "What happens if you visit several countries in one trip before flying home?" |
| CUSTOMER: | "I can only have one chip installed, so I have to choose whichever country I am going to be in for the longest duration." |
| SALES PRO: | "How do you handle mobile communication for the other countries you are visiting? Are there any countries you visit for which your current telephone provider doesn't offer a chip?" |
| CUSTOMER: | "I have to purchase a prepaid telephone when I arrive at each country and, yes, there are many countries that I visit where I cannot use my own mobile phone." |
| SALES PRO: | "So currently before you travel, you have to visit the store, wait for the chip to be installed and, if you are visiting many countries in one trip, make sure that the chip is for the country where you will stay for the longest period. For the countries where you don't have access to your phone, you have to purchase a prepaid phone, call your company, friends and family to make them aware of your new temporary telephone number and, when you get back, reconcile all the different invoices for the telephones you've purchased?" |
| CUSTOMER: | "That's correct." |
| SALES PRO: | "Mr. Smith, if I could offer you a telephone that would give you the ability to make and receive calls in any country in the world without having to visit a store for chip installation before your trip and enable you to use your own telephone number regardless of what country you were in, would that be an advantage?" |

CUSTOMER:     "Of course."

SALES PRO:    "This mobile phone incorporates different technology than any other phone. It has a specific chip built into it that offers an eight-way communication system, which connects with every current provider and network system in the world. This would mean that you would be able to use the phone in any country you visit, thus eliminating the hassle of purchasing new phones with different telephone numbers. Your family or company could call your local telephone number and reach you regardless of the country you are visiting, and you would never have to plan your trip as it relates to telephone communications again."

Thanks to correct questioning, the knowledge of his product and the realization that his competition could not offer the same feature on its mobile phones, the salesperson was able to match the criteria his customer said was important and then set new criteria with the exclusive chip.

Your focus should always be on what you or your company have identified as your existing differentiators. However, sometimes the newest eyes are the brightest, so as you capture more time with potential customers and become more knowledgeable about your product, your competition and your specific industry, you may be inspired by an epiphany that you can present to your manager, the marketing department or the owner that creates more differentiation. To ask the question "What if?" can trigger a new thought that increases the company's ability to broaden their market or establish a new application that hasn't yet been considered. That new thought could be an intuitive function that doesn't currently exist, automation that is currently manual, or smoother aesthetics that create better ergonomics, reduced size or dramatically increased speed, all of which offer further value for customers and potential profitability for your company.

The earlier you can establish yourself as a creative thinker, the more you will set yourself apart from other sales people. Both your manager and her manager will appreciate your passion and creative thought process and give you immediate recognition as an advanced sales person. For example, it was a sales rookie selling copiers who noted that "All of our competitors focus on speed.

I understand from my training that we offer superior copy-quality accuracy, so why don't we focus on the superior accuracy of our copy quality in addition to the speed?" This simple question triggered the owners to complete a lengthy review of the facts that would allow them to justify the statement, which led to a new sales training and marketing campaign focused on the importance of copy-quality accuracy in addition to speed, separating the company further from the competition.

## Creating Differentiation

If after further review you determine you don't have product or company differentiation, you will be relying heavily on the benefits you do have to offer and the relationships with your clients; your value proposition may be price driven. More often than not, you can create a potential differentiator by taking an in-depth look at your existing product or company to establish whether you have one or two significant features that your competition also has—but is not highlighting. An emphasis on the benefits and results of these specific features can be just as powerful a differentiator, especially if your cost is more affordable and you have the opportunity to personally present these features. Your company culture and philosophy can also be used as primary differentiators, serving as reasons for a potential customer to use *your* product instead of your competitor's.

Simply adding a service that the competition does not have or taking away a restriction that is causing a problem could also result in more sales. For example, it was another sales rookie working as a fitness trainer who became so frustrated by the number of people who didn't turn up for their appointments or use their membership that the trainer decided to personally research why. Two problems were identified: a lack of self-motivation and transportation problems. The trainer's epiphany was to create two additional features that could be used to attract new members: early-morning wake-up calls for clients and a company minibus service to pick up clients and take them back home.

It usually doesn't take long before one of your competitors catches on and establishes a new product or company option that is equal or similar to the differentiation you currently offer. Since differentiation doesn't last forever, take advantage of what currently separates you from the competition. The results you achieve will speak for themselves.

# SELLING
# THE SIZZLE

CARTOON STORY

I JUST HEARD A COMPARISON TO HELP ME SELL THE RESULT OF MY PRODUCT BENEFITS — WANT TO HEAR?

OKAY!

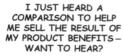

SELL THE SIZZLE - NOT THE STEAK!

THAT'S GREAT! YOU MEAN SELL THE SMELL AND THE TASTE, NOT JUST THE MEAT.

EXACTLY. I'VE GOT ANOTHER ONE — SELL THE VIEW, NOT THE WINDOW.

YES, BUT ULTIMATELY THE REASON THE CUSTOMER WANTS THE WINDOW IS FOR THE VIEW OR THE LIGHT. THE OTHER BENEFITS MENTIONED WILL GIVE THEM MAINTENANCE-FREE WINDOWS IN THE FUTURE, WHICH WILL MEAN MORE TIME TO ENJOY DOING OTHER THINGS AS WELL AS LESS EXPENSE.

EXCELLENT. IN FACT, I KNOW SOMEONE WHO SELLS WINDOWS. HE WAS TAUGHT TO SELL THE THICK DOUBLE-PANED GLASS, THE SPECIAL MOLDED PLASTIC AND THE BACK-UP WARRANTY.

I SEE, AND THE THICK DOUBLE PANED GLASS WILL GIVE THEM MORE COMFORTABLE LIVING CONDITIONS, AND THE WARRANTY WILL GIVE THEM PEACE OF MIND AGAINST ANY WINDOW PROBLEMS IN THE FUTURE.

# THREE

# The Sales Cycle

## Sales Cycle Personality

A sales cycle is the average amount of time it takes before you would expect a decision from your potential customer. The length of time is usually dictated by the number of people involved in the decision-making process and the size of the investment. Products with a short sales cycle usually require a decision on the first or second call and involve only one or two decision makers. Products that require a long sales cycle will involve building relationships with the decision makers and with those who could influence the decision due to their involvement in the usage of the product. Additionally, with long sales cycles you might have technicians, engineers or IT people on your sales team who are required to capture information from your customer and recommend a solution for you to present.

Sales pros utilize their character traits to their advantage, and I've found they usually choose the type of sales cycle that suits them best. If you are an individual with intense energy, little patience, a need for instant gratification and very strong sales drive, you will be happier selling products with a short sales cycle. If you are methodical and patient, however, and enjoy building long-term relationships, you will be better suited for selling products and services with a longer sales cycle.

I first realized how different the objectives and sales techniques were in selling products that had a short sales cycle as opposed to those with a long sales cycle after my first business-to-business sales appointment. The sales cycle for my first sales position selling insulation to homeowners, which had given me so much success, was extremely short and commonly known as the one-call close. The first appointment was also the presentation, and if you didn't close the customer on the presentation, you rarely got a sale. As experienced as I was, walking into that first appointment, I couldn't have been any more naïve with the sales approach I was aiming to use with my second sales position, in which I was selling to corporations and not homeowners.

My new company sold mailing and shipping systems that allowed a company to automate their mailing and compare rates for different carriers when shipping parcels and packages. One week after joining, and with a full week's product training behind me, I found myself on my first appointment, which was a referral from one of my previous customers. We had a two-day break before the strategic sales training, so I positioned the appointment before the next training was to start. With my ego still following me from the success of my first sales position, my thought was to hit the ground running, just like I had before, and walk into the next phase of training with my very first order. What a reality check I got!

The appointment was at 10 a.m., and although I was nervous walking into the unfamiliar territory of a corporate company instead of a home, I was as prepared as I could be with all the product information from my training. Ten minutes after I signed in, the conference door opened and four people walked in and handed me their respective business cards. My referral contact introduced himself and, after a brief introduction, got straight to business asking me questions that were focused not on products but on the strategic aspect of how we could integrate a logistics system that would offer real-time communication to all their branch locations. Each person had questions that related to their specific division, and I had no idea how to answer any of them. After fifteen minutes, the first of the four excused herself for another appointment; five minutes later I was walking out the door. When I left the appointment I looked at the business cards to find that the person I had been referred to was the CFO; the other three were the director of logistics, VP of sales and director of marketing.

Needless to say I was out of my depth with no clear idea of what direction to take the appointment. Based on my previous sales experience, I had expected to meet with one person, ask my questions, show my product and, when the customer inevitably asked if I could deliver in three weeks, say, "If I can, will you move forward?"

Although we offered a breadth of products, some small enough to allow for a quick decision, I had found myself in front of a very large opportunity that had obviously caught me off guard. It turned out they were looking for a new logistics system to connect all their offices using a seamless integrated shipping system that would offer real-time manifesting to specific carriers and create sales statistics reports. As you can imagine, this type of opportunity was not a one-call close!

That day I learned the valuable lesson that sales skills and experience, no matter how valuable in one company, do not always dictate success in another. Therefore, always ensure you fully comprehend every aspect of the sales cycle you are involved in: the decision makers and potential influencers, the expected time frame for a decision and, if you have an internal team, what their responsibilities are and what you can expect from them.

In addition to identifying which sales cycle suits your personality, you should understand the difference in the sales techniques according to the sales cycle for your product or service. Although the majority of sales techniques are used for both cycles, there is a fundamental difference in what your objectives will be, when you incorporate these strategies into the sales process, how you position them and the response you can expect to receive from your customer. Achieving a final commitment for a large-volume sale requires patience and techniques that are focused heavily on asking questions and gathering information throughout all stages of the sales process. Large sales also require a thorough understanding of the value proposition you are going to offer, and hinge on your ability to build relationships with all the relevant decision makers and influencers. Compared to small sales, large sales require much more knowledge of the competition, of the potential customer's buying process, of the customer's criteria for buying and of how to set the new criteria.

The strategies and techniques that match a specific sales cycle will become apparent as you read through the book; however, following are a few basic facts to be aware of, especially as it relates to closing the sale.

One-call commitment techniques are perfect for small-volume sales if the expectation is for your potential customer to make a snap decision; perhaps she is the only decision maker, or the decision doesn't require significant investment. However, the same techniques will have a detrimental effect if they are used on potential customers in situations where your product requires a longer sales cycle due to the number of decision makers or the size of the financial investment.

Longer sales cycles require obtaining commitments through each stage of the sale; often you must test what you have presented, meet with another influencer or acquire financial information to create a cost comparison. Larger sales require you to comprehensively use every communication technique presented in *The Sales Pro* with the realization that the final decision will be based on all the information and stage-by-stage commitments incorporated into your final presentation.

The stage-by-stage commitments are confirmed by your ability to prequalify each specific point. Prequalifying enables you to ask your customers if they are in agreement with what you have just said, or it could be a question you ask that reconfirms your customer's situation before you offer a possible solution. For example, you might ask one influencer if he is in agreement with what you have just presented, and if he confirms yes, prequalify him further by asking if he would refer you to others who could also influence the decision. However, in the case of a product with a short sales cycle, a prequalification would usually consist of a question that when positively answered confirms your customer is moving forward with the sale.

## Building Rapport

In addition to adapting your techniques to match the sales cycle of the product you are selling, you should also be aware of how to build rapport during your interactions with your potential customer. This skill is especially important to master if you are selling a product with a short sales cycle, since you have a limited amount of time to build this relationship.

Building rapport with your potential customer creates immediate connection and becomes the platform on which your business relationship will progress. Sales pros understand their customer's viewpoint and have an incredible ability to be humble yet confident, which automatically makes them very likeable. Make sure you are putting yourself in your customer's position. During your conversations with your prospective customers, be aware of their verbal tone and style of talking in addition to their body language. If you can reflect these subconscious signals, you can likely win them over without their even realizing what you've done.

For example, if you are selling to professional businessmen, you should talk in their language, using similar vocabulary to that of their profession, act formally and dress in a similar manner. However, if you're talking to builders, shift your style from that of the businessmen to the style of the builders, perhaps dressing and speaking more casually. Copy their stance, the tone of their voice and their energy level, especially when discussing serious points such as money. It's fine to be excited and passionate about your product when presenting, but when the conversation changes to more serious issues, that's where the reflection of your customer is most important.

Never rush when talking with your potential customer, and always maintain the customer's pace. Prospective customers should command your complete attention. Your focus should remain on them at all times, and not on the customer you will be seeing afterward. It is far better to do all you can to progress the current sale than to give a half-hearted, rushed effort to get to the next appointment. Remember, people buy people first."

Make sure you are likeable by listening, observing and responding to what customers are saying, showing you have their interest at heart. If they are hurried, impatient or looking in another direction, stop what you're saying and ask a question, change the direction of your questions or simply ask if you have caught them at a bad time. Are they truly listening to what you are saying? Have you explained why you are asking questions or the purpose of your call?

Use names as regularly as you can, as such action shows confidence and sincerity. Many mediocre salespeople spend twice as much time talking as they do listening! Not only do they miss opportunities to progress the sale, but they lose their credibility with the customer too.

Master the following list of advice on building rapport and you'll be on your way to a quick transition to a true sales pro.

**Building Rapport**

- Maintain regular eye contact with your customer.

- Put yourself in your customer's position.

- Listen and respond accordingly.

- Don't be pushy.

- Acknowledge your customer's concerns.

- Relate to your customer's company and current circumstances.

- Maintain a similar level of energy.

- Be respectful, regardless of your client's status or size of the sale.

- Focus on your customer's emotions.

- Offer ideas.

- Don't overstay your welcome.

- Use your customer's industry terms.

# THE BIG PICTURE

CARTOON STORY

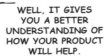

JOHN, WHAT'S THE BENEFIT OF SEEING WHERE YOUR PRODUCT OR SERVICE FITS INTO THE WHOLE PICTURE OF THE COMPANY YOU'RE SELLING TO?

WELL, IT GIVES YOU A BETTER UNDERSTANDING OF HOW YOUR PRODUCT WILL HELP.

IT ALSO HELPS TO SHOW YOU HOW THE BENEFITS OF YOUR PRODUCT OR SERVICE WILL AFFECT OTHER AREAS WITHIN THE COMPANY.

I THINK I SEE WHAT YOU MEAN, BUT CAN YOU GIVE ME AN EXAMPLE?

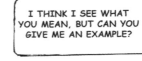

WELL, YOU MAY BE PRESENTING YOUR SERVICE TO THE HEAD OF THE ACCOUNTS DEPARTMENT, SHOWING THEM HOW THEY WILL BENEFIT BY USING YOUR SERVICE. HOWEVER, WHEN YOUR SERVICE IS USED, THE MARKETING DEPARTMENT MAY ALSO BENEFIT TOO.

AND ADDS MORE WEIGHT TO YOUR SALE, MAKING IT EASIER TO JUSTIFY.

# FOUR

# Effective Questioning Techniques

A sales pro understands that every aspect of the sales process incorporates questions; the right question presented in the correct way at the right time will open up sales opportunities that the average salesperson does not see. Sales pros make it their job to ask a "mix" of questions, ensuring that their customers feel like they are having a conversation, oblivious to the fact that they are giving information away that the salesperson is able to use to progress or close the sale. Specific questions and questioning techniques that relate to particular areas of the sales process are incorporated into each chapter of this book.

The techniques presented in this chapter are a reinforcement of the basic types of questions that sales pros employ.

## Open and Closed Questions

Two types of questions are open and closed. A closed question prompts either a "yes" or "no" answer while an open question ensures that your prospect responds in a more detailed manner.

The important point to remember is not to analyze which type of question you are asking, but to offer more than just statements. A statement is simply a sentence that does not invite a response. However, a statement can be used effectively to either regain or put focus on a particular area of concern or interest.

It's also important to position your questions so that you get emotional responses; this is achieved by changing keywords like "think" to "feel."

Below are examples of open questions, closed questions and statements.

## Open Questions

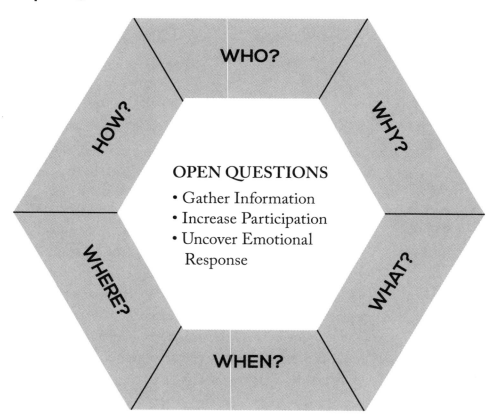

Open questions are used to invite a more detailed response than just yes or no. These usually start with *who, why, what, when, where,* or *how.* Open questions are used when we want to gather information, increase participation or uncover an emotional response.

Examples include:

- "Why did you choose your existing product?"
- "What would happen if your existing product broke down?"
- "Where would you be using the product?"
- "How do you currently review whether your existing product is cost effective?"

To uncover an emotional response, use "feel" instead of "think."

- "What do you **think** about the new product?"
- "How do you **feel** about the new product?"

As you communicate with your customer listen to the words she is using and capture her communication style. For example, if she is saying "That looks really good" or "Can you show me what you mean?" you would have identified a visual communicator; however, if she is using words like "Can you say that again?" or "How does the engine sound?" she is more of an auditory communicator.

If you have identified that your potential customer is more of a visual communicator, you could change your questions to:

- "How does that **look** to you?"
- "Where do you **see** the product fitting in?"

If you've identified an auditory communicator, you could change your questions to:

- "How does that **sound** to you?"
- "Let me share what some of our customers are **saying**."
- "I **hear** what you are saying."

## Closed Questions

Closed questions are used to confirm agreement, check understanding, gain attention, clarify a point, check interest or change the direction of a conversation. For example: "I agree. Can you see how that will help?" Closed questions are also used to "close the doors" after explaining a particular point or feature; for example, "Have you any questions about that?" This method ensures that the prospect understands and has no questions about the point you just made. This eliminates the chances that you will be presenting the next point with the prospect still thinking about your previous comments. Additional examples of closed questions include:

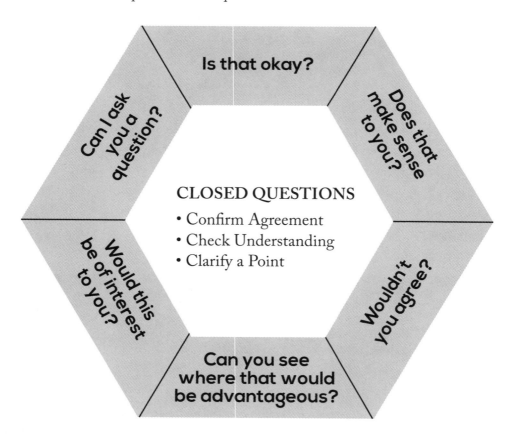

Is that okay?

Can I ask you a question?

Does that make sense to you?

CLOSED QUESTIONS
• Confirm Agreement
• Check Understanding
• Clarify a Point

Would this be of interest to you?

Wouldn't you agree?

Can you see where that would be advantageous?

## Statements

Statements are used to offer an explanation or to present something that does not require a response. A closed question can follow a statement. You can use a statement to clarify a point or lay the foundation for a future question you want to ask. Examples include:

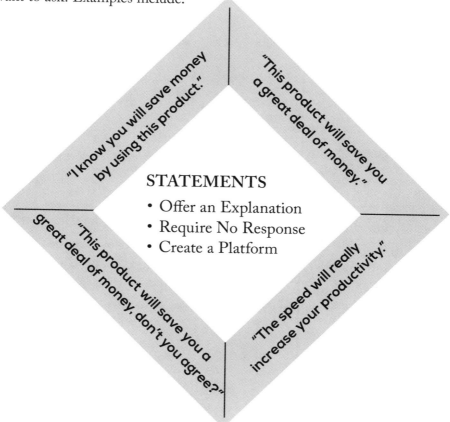

"I know you will save money by using this product."

"This product will save you a great deal of money."

**STATEMENTS**
- Offer an Explanation
- Require No Response
- Create a Platform

"This product will save you a great deal of money, don't you agree?"

"The speed will really increase your productivity."

Below is an example of a statement made to clarify a point and lay the foundation for later questions.

"You mentioned that increasing the speed of your existing product would help reduce the amount of money currently spent shipping your products to your customers. I'd like to understand more about your current shipping method."

## Flip Questioning

To flip a question is to answer a question with a question. This powerful tool creates more time to think about a possible answer to a question you have been asked. It's used effectively in the political arena when a politician either wants to avoid a question or does not have an immediate answer. For example:

CUSTOMER:        "How much does it cost?"

SALES PRO:        "How much would you expect it to cost?"


CUSTOMER:        "Why should I change?"

SALES PRO:        "Why shouldn't you?"


Be careful with this technique; in order to be effective, it must be used in conjunction with the right attitude, voice tone, and body language. The right attitude would mean asking the question not to be clever but to open up further dialogue that will help your customer make a decision. The right voice tone would be asking the question without force or assertion and your body language would reflect a relaxed conversational demeanor with a hint of a smile.

## Tagalong Questions

Sales pros intuitively capture important information by asking tagalong questions. A tagalong question follows the same direction as the initial questions you ask your potential customer. The purpose of such questions is to find out more information on the same subject as the initial questions, going deeper to reveal more details.

The problem with many sales people is they just ask initial questions, which means losing out on so much information. The answers from the tagalong questions actually give you the most information, thus enabling you to close more appointments and progress more sales.

Following are two examples of a salesperson trying to sell a photocopying machine to a businessman. Example one shows the sales person asking only initial questions, and example two shows the sales pro asking the same initial questions as well as tagalong questions. To understand the full effect and power of asking tagalong questions, take these examples and role-play with a friend. Act out the role of both the salesperson and the prospective customer. As you will find out, in the salesperson's position, you are getting much more information with such questions, and will feel much more effective at your job. As the prospective customer, you will feel as though you are in the hands of a professional who actually cares about your answers.

> **Example One:**
>
> **Initial Question:** "Do you ever have more than one original document to copy at one time?"
>
> **Second Question:** "Does your existing photocopier offer a reduction facility?"

The first example shows a sales person who asks two initial questions and is about to ask several more, all completely different from each other.

This is the common trait of a new salesperson, who usually isn't even taking the time to listen to the answers; he just wants to get to the point where he is presenting his company's photocopier to the prospective customer.

Can you see the mistake? If he had also asked the tagalong questions as in example two he could learn much more from the initial questions. The answers to the tagalong questions provide deeper, more valuable information on each point, that can then be used to progress the sale.

Example Two:

**Initial Question:** "Do you ever have more than one original document to copy at one time?"

Tagalong Question: "How often?"

Tagalong Question: "How long does it usually take?"

Tagalong Question: "Do you ever get interrupted?"

Tagalong Question: "What do you do then?"

**Second Question:** "Does your existing photocopier offer a reduction facility?"

Tagalong Question: "How often do you use it?"

Tagalong Question: "What do you reduce?"

Tagalong Question: "What's the quality like when it's reduced?"

# TAGALONG QUESTIONS

CARTOON STORY

## The Reflecting Technique

Sales pros engage in "reflecting," which means being aware of the buyer's view and of your own. Reflecting ensures that the solution you are going to present matches what the customer needs—and if it doesn't match, this technique gives you the ability to acknowledge what the customer has asked for so that you can effectively explain why you are recommending an alternative.

The reflecting technique, which will confirm to your customer that you fully understand the desired end result and are both on the same page, incorporates seven steps that should be taken before you present your product. These seven steps are:

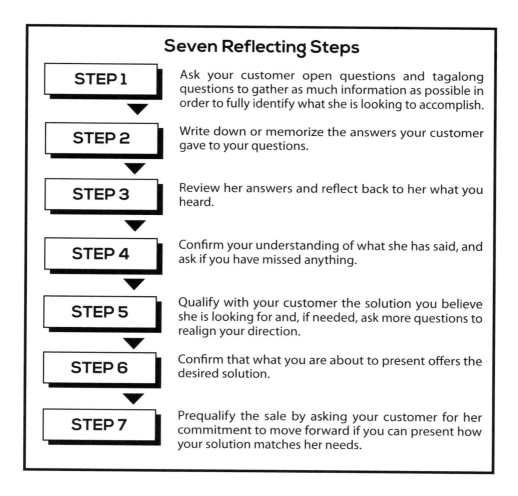

### Seven Reflecting Steps

**STEP 1** — Ask your customer open questions and tagalong questions to gather as much information as possible in order to fully identify what she is looking to accomplish.

**STEP 2** — Write down or memorize the answers your customer gave to your questions.

**STEP 3** — Review her answers and reflect back to her what you heard.

**STEP 4** — Confirm your understanding of what she has said, and ask if you have missed anything.

**STEP 5** — Qualify with your customer the solution you believe she is looking for and, if needed, ask more questions to realign your direction.

**STEP 6** — Confirm that what you are about to present offers the desired solution.

**STEP 7** — Prequalify the sale by asking your customer for her commitment to move forward if you can present how your solution matches her needs.

Sales pros are able to memorize the answers they receive from their customers while they continue to ask questions, which makes this technique even more powerful due to the natural, conversational interaction between the sales pro and the customer. A sales person should always use a tablet computer or a notepad to capture information until his comfort level and confidence in front of customers allow him to progress to memorization. Don't worry if you memorize or write down the information incorrectly when you begin to use this technique. It is far better to be authentic and reconfirm the answer to a question to ensure you are offering the right solution; your prospective customer will appreciate your thoroughness.

If at any stage you don't quite understand what your prospective customer has said or is asking for, ask her to clarify. Too many people are afraid to show they do not understand the other person's point or thoughts. You will sell far more by admitting your confusion than you ever will by pretending.

## Practice Your Technique

It is best to learn the reflecting technique one step at a time. Practice with someone by giving him some information and then ask him to repeat it back to you. You'll be amazed at how little he had originally taken in or how inaccurate he is.

First ask questions, and then write the information you receive back on a notepad or enter it into your electronic tablet. Once you have mastered the art of writing exactly what the other person has said and verbally confirming it, practice looking at the information you have written to qualify which benefits of your product will benefit the customer. Once you know the benefits you are going to present, confirm that what you are about to present does offer the solution he is looking for, and then prequalify the sale by asking for his commitment if your solution matches his needs. Do your best to maintain eye contact while you listen and take notes; this adds credibility and authenticity. The more you practice, the more effective you will become.

## Alignment with Prospective Customers

Once you have mastered the art of memorizing the information, reflecting back what you heard, confirming your understanding of the information and qualifying how your product will benefit your prospective customer—all while continuing to talk and listen—you will have progressed further toward the status of a true sales pro. Interacting with your prospective customer involves thinking on your feet, communicating effectively and remaining "sharp." The better you get at reflecting, the quicker you will be able to size up a situation and establish immediate rapport and credibility with your customer.

With the reflecting technique, you are gathering information, analyzing it, comparing it to information you have already heard or experienced, and computing an answer. Sometimes you can be off base—and totally unaware of it. Your prospective customer may have one idea or expectation in his mind and you have another.

That's why it's good to express to your prospective customer the way you see his problem or situation. If it is not established that your reflections are the same, your prospective customer will grow bored and frustrated. You'll be confused by his lack of interest and, in the end, are bound to get the response, "I'll have to think about it."

## When Visions Don't Match

To understand how detrimental it is when the prospective customer and the salesperson do not share the same vision, imagine the following scenario.

As you walk into a hairdressing salon, the hairdresser greets you with a smile and takes you to a chair.

Before you sit down, he asks you a couple of questions and says, "I know what you want. Let's get your hair washed." He looks professional to you, you've told him what you want, and he is representing himself as a professional stylist, so you go along with it. You might even feel it would be embarrassing not to comply.

As he starts cutting your hair, you become a little nervous because he's either talking too much, constantly being distracted by other people, or the conversation indicates that he may not know what he is doing. When he tells you he's finished, you look in the mirror to see a different cut than you asked for! It's too late for any changes now.

The stylist's reflection of what you asked for was not accurate. Don't be the salesperson who, like the stylist, rushes straight into his presentation without establishing beforehand that the result he has in mind is the same as that of his prospective customer.

Now consider the example of another professional stylist. You walk into this different hairdressing salon six months later. You are wary about getting your hair cut, and you've requested the top stylist. The stylist comes over and starts with a consultation. She asks questions, listens to what you have to say, and then continues to ask more questions.

After listening carefully, the stylist reflects back what she feels you're looking for. She says, "The way I see it, you want the length to be just below your shoulders, but the back slightly shorter than the sides. You want the sides curved toward your face and a parting textured into your hair from the right." At this stage, you have the option to correct the stylist until you feel the stylist understands exactly what you're looking for.

The stylist listened to you and demonstrated that she is interested in cutting your hair correctly. If the stylist feels the style would not be suitable, she can then explain to you why she feels this way and recommend another style that is more suitable (and which will also leave you happy). By communicating that something else could be more appropriate, the stylist reconfirms that she has a real interest in you.

The stylist gets a hair book and points to the style you agree to, which adds to the stylist's credibility and professionalism. It shows she cares

enough to take as much time as needed and ask as many questions as necessary. This puts your mind at ease and increases your confidence in the result.

This stylist asked good questions, listened, reflected back what you said and added her own experienced opinion. Happy with your new style and with the entire experience, you're likely to return for future haircuts and even tell others about the stylist. By creating an effective communication channel, both parties end up pleased and confident.

## Basic Communication

So what does this scenario have to do with sales? Think of selling as basic communication. The reflecting technique the stylist used can be compared to a professional salesperson who listens to what the prospective customer is asking for, reflects back what he has just heard to confirm the reflections are the same, responds accordingly with his prospective customer's interest in mind, gives another option if necessary, explains why, and leads into the presentation. When a salesperson uses basic communication to confirm a shared vision, the customer feels he is in capable hands and dealing with a real professional.

# REFLECTING

CARTOON STORY

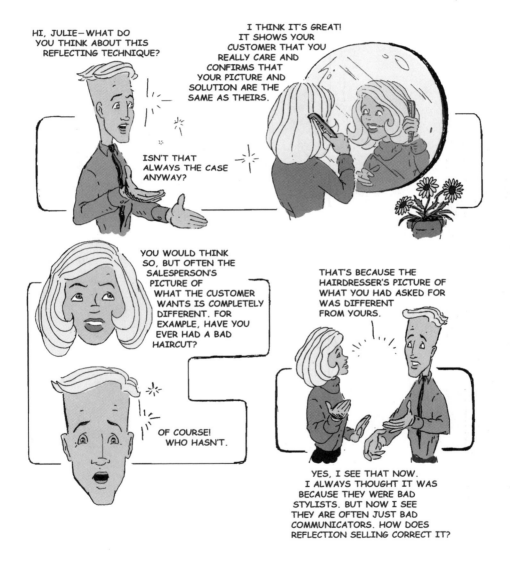

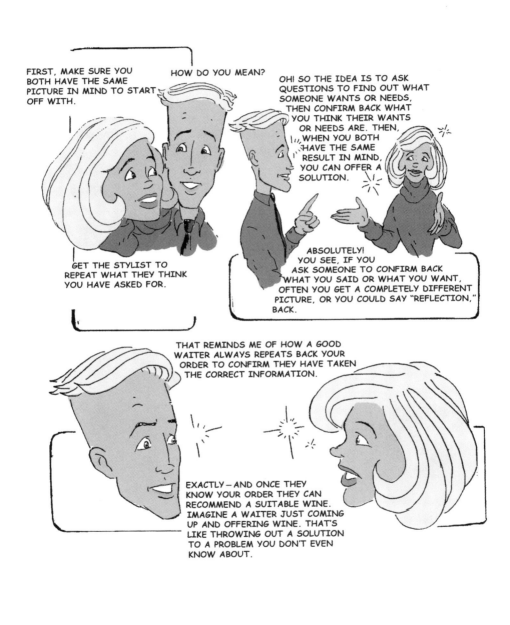

# FIVE

# The Strategic Law of Numbers

### Review the Numbers

The law of numbers will be one of the sales person's best motivators. It's an average of all your activity and sales figures over a period of time: monthly or quarterly and year to date. The results identify how you are progressing and, if your company measures sales statistics, how you compare to your company averages.

The average indicates areas where you need to focus to increase your results, such as setting more appointments, closing more orders or increasing your order value. It helps to analyze exactly what the facts are with regard to your results. For example, many sales people who are not closing orders often learn that it isn't their closing techniques, their presentation, their product or their attitude; after analyzing their problem, they realize they've been presenting to people who did not have the authority to make a decision even if they wanted to. (Perhaps they were presenting to an influencer or a person who was given the task of collecting information or meeting with salespeople.) This situation could be prevented by prequalifying what part the person you are meeting with will play in the decision-making process.

Analyzing your past results gives you valuable information to help favorably affect your results in the future. A sales pro will always analyze past experiences and results so he can quickly redefine his focus and meet his financial goals. Ask yourself the following questions when analyzing your sales performance:

- What activities create appointments for me?
- How much time did I spend on new appointment activities today/this week?
- How many new calls did I make today?
- How many calls were to existing users?
- How many calls were to new users?
- How many appointments did I set?
- How many actual presentations did I complete?
- How many presentations were made to decision makers?
- How many sales did I get?
- How much was my total business?

Sales is often associated with risk; yet if you understand the law of numbers, you will realize that little risk is actually involved. As long as you make so many calls, you will make so many appointments, and then sell so many products that will in turn produce a commission or bonus for you. The more knowledgeable you become in your products, in the competition and in applying the sales techniques, the more products you will sell to the same number of people. The more people you contact, the more money you will earn. It usually takes about three months to establish your personal averages. After that time you can establish areas where you are doing well and areas where you can improve.

To establish your averages, consider the following ratios:

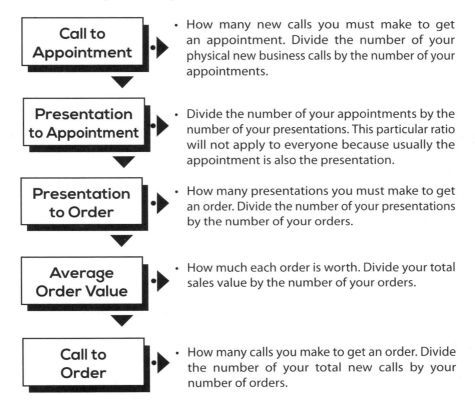

**Call to Appointment**
- How many new calls you must make to get an appointment. Divide the number of your physical new business calls by the number of your appointments.

**Presentation to Appointment**
- Divide the number of your appointments by the number of your presentations. This particular ratio will not apply to everyone because usually the appointment is also the presentation.

**Presentation to Order**
- How many presentations you must make to get an order. Divide the number of your presentations by the number of your orders.

**Average Order Value**
- How much each order is worth. Divide your total sales value by the number of your orders.

**Call to Order**
- How many calls you make to get an order. Divide the number of your total new calls by your number of orders.

There are many other averages you can establish, and you can also go into more detail with the averages you have. For example, the new business calls ratio could be further defined by establishing which calls were telephone calls, which were to existing customers, how many were first-time calls, and how many were second- or third-time calls.

It's smart to keep it simple, however. The above ratios are the main averages that will be immediately useful to you. The beauty of analyzing your results is that you will not only learn where you can improve, but you will also see what you are doing right.

For example, you may be making ten calls to get an appointment, and every fourth appointment you are making a sale. You can then calculate that for every forty calls you make, you will get an order.

Let's say that the value of your average order is $3,000 and you are paid 15 percent on your sales volume. You now expect that for every forty calls you make, you will be paid a $450 commission. If you then divide the $450 by the forty calls you had to make, you can see that every time you made a new call, you were paid $11.25, even if the person shut the door in your face or hung up the phone.

You can now determine how much you want to earn by deciding how hard you want to work. Once you start analyzing your results, review potential options to increase your success. You may realize that if you add another package to your existing product, it will also increase your average order value, which in turn will increase your commission.

Consider the following example of a salesperson's figures at the end of a month:

| Sales Ratios | | | | | | | |
|---|---|---|---|---|---|---|---|
| | New Calls | Appointments | Call to Appointment | Number of Sales | Sale to Appointment | Revenue | Average Order Value |
| Month Total | 475 | 40 | New Calls Divided by Appointments = 11.8 Calls to Achieve an Appointment | 8 | Appointments Divided by Number of Sales = 5 Appointments to Achieve a Sale | $48,000 | Revenue Divided by Number of Sales = $6,000 |

The call-to-appointment ratio would be 475 divided by forty, which equals one appointment for every 11.87 new business calls made. The presentation-to-order ratio would be forty presentations divided by eight sales, which equals one sale for every five presentations. If you divide the monthly order value of $48,000 by eight sales, it will equal an average order of $6,000.

Compare this with your previous month's results to see your progress. Then add these numbers to your totals from the previous months of the year to get your year-to-date figures.

## Increasing Sales

There are two ways to increase your sales results: Make more calls, or become more productive on the calls you are making. More productive could mean increasing your average order size by selling additional services or supplies, increasing your knowledge on the competition so you can more easily justify the reason to change or learning more about how to position financing for your product to facilitate an easier buying decision for customers who haven't budgeted the money.

The figures will show you where you need to improve. For example, you may learn that you are getting one sale for every seven appointments and your goal is to achieve one sale for every four appointments. This means that either you are not presenting to the decision makers or that you need to improve your presenting, closing or questioning skills. By using the ratios, you can quickly identify what you need to focus on.

Regardless of your experience, you should constantly strive to improve your presentation skills in order to achieve more effective results from each day. If you do not try to improve, your results will stay the same, and if you become discouraged, your efforts will falter and you will earn less money.

The decision is yours. If you keep doing what you've been doing, you're going to keep getting what you've been getting. The better you get and the more knowledgeable you become, the more your conversion rates will improve. In turn, your earnings will increase.

## Sales Ratios

| Week | New Calls | Appointments | Call to Appointment | Number of Sales | Sale to Appointment | Revenue | Average Order Value |
|---|---|---|---|---|---|---|---|
| 1 | | | | | | | |
| 2 | | | | | | | |
| 3 | | | | | | | |
| 4 | | | | | | | |
| 5 | | | | | | | |
| TOTAL | | | | | | | |
| 1 | | | | | | | |
| 2 | | | | | | | |
| 3 | | | | | | | |
| 4 | | | | | | | |
| 5 | | | | | | | |
| TOTAL | | | | | | | |
| 1 | | | | | | | |
| 2 | | | | | | | |
| 3 | | | | | | | |
| 4 | | | | | | | |
| 5 | | | | | | | |
| TOTAL | | | | | | | |
| 1 | | | | | | | |
| 2 | | | | | | | |
| 3 | | | | | | | |
| 4 | | | | | | | |
| 5 | | | | | | | |
| TOTAL | | | | | | | |
| MONTH TOTAL | | | | | | | |

# LAW OF NUMBERS

CARTOON STORY

HI, PETE. HOW ARE YOU DOING WITH YOUR NEW SALES POSITION?

LAW OF NUMBERS? WHAT DO YOU MEAN?

GREAT! I WAS CONCERNED AT FIRST AFTER ALL THE STORIES PEOPLE HAD TOLD ME ABOUT IT BEING RISKY BUT THEN I LEARNED ABOUT THE LAW OF NUMBERS AND NOW I NEVER HAVE ANY WORRY.

IT'S AN AVERAGE OF HOW MANY CALLS YOU HAVE TO MAKE TO GET AN APPOINTMENT, AND THEN HOW MANY APPOINTMENTS YOU WOULD NORMALLY HAVE TO DO TO GET A SALE.

YOU MEAN, AS LONG AS YOU DO THE CALLS, EVERYTHING ELSE TAKES CARE OF ITSELF?

YES, OBVIOUSLY YOUR ATTITUDE HAS TO BE RIGHT, BUT THE EXCITING THING IS, THE BETTER AND MORE EXPERIENCED YOU GET, THE MORE RESULTS YOU GET FROM THE SAME NUMBER OF CALLS.

SO WHAT ARE YOUR AVERAGES THEN?

WELL, OVER THE PAST THREE MONTHS SINCE I STARTED, I HAVE MADE AN APPOINTMENT EVERY 16 CALLS, AND FOR EVERY 6 APPOINTMENTS I DO, I GET A SALE. AT THE MOMENT I GET 10% COMMISSION ON WHATEVER I SELL, AND MY AVERAGE ORDER IS $4,000.

HMM,

LAST MONTH I MADE 600 CALLS. I GOT 37 APPOINTMENTS AND MADE 6 SALES.

SO IF YOU MADE 6 SALES AND YOUR AVERAGE ORDER VALUE IS $4,000, THAT MEANS YOU SOLD $24,000 WORTH OF BUSINESS.

YES, AND AT 10%, I GOT $2,400 IN COMMISSION!

THAT'S GOOD MONEY... AND YOU'RE ON COMMISSION ONLY, AREN'T YOU?

YES, AND I WOULDN'T HAVE IT ANY OTHER WAY. NOW THAT I HAVE LEARNED ABOUT AVERAGES, THERE IS NEVER ANY NEED FOR CONCERN UNLESS I FEEL LAZY, AND THEN THAT'S MY OWN PERSONAL DUTY TO PICK MYSELF UP AGAIN. PLUS, THE BETTER I GET AT REFINING MY SALES TECHNIQUES, THE MORE EFFECTIVE I BECOME. I KNOW OUR TOP SALESPERSON MAKES JUST AS MANY CALLS AS ME, YET EARNS A LOT MORE MONEY!

WHY IS THAT?

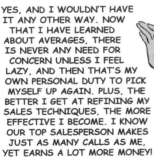

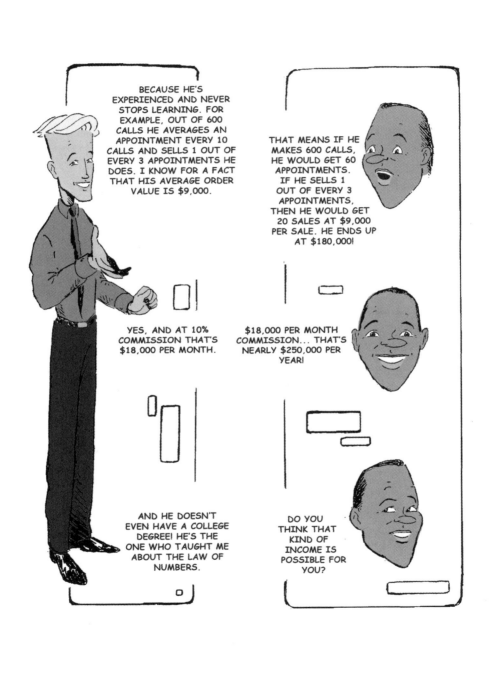

# SIX

# The Key to New Business Development

Most sales people start their sales career in a new business development role, which is, without doubt, the best training ground for not just testing your character but also learning more about customer interaction, the competition and refining the selling skills you have been taught. Where you are going to focus, what you do when you focus and who the people are within a company to focus on are essential factors in how effective you will be with your time. You'll need to have a clear understanding of who you need to talk to and what the objective will be from each conversation.

For example, you'll need to know how to quickly ascertain if you are speaking with a potential decision maker, an influencer or an information gatherer (a person who cannot make the decision or influence it).

## Identify Major Players

The sales pro makes it his job to ensure he meets and uncovers information from all the major players in the prospective company—the users of the product and the influencers who will benefit from what the sales pro is offering before he meets with the decision maker. He knows inherently whom he needs to meet with and what to ask in order to uncover information that will help to justify an appointment when he meets or talks with the decision maker(s). The decision maker appreciates this approach because she knows the sales pro has a good understanding of their current situation and will have a valid reason as to why they should meet.

An inexperienced sales person will often make the mistake of not uncovering information from the users and influencers and instead ask questions directly to the decision maker. A decision maker expects you to have done your homework and will be frustrated if he thinks you are taking up his time asking questions that could have been answered by his employees. Therefore, make sure you ask your questions to the relevant people who use the product or can influence the decision before speaking with the decision maker directly.

For example, let's say you are a corporate salesperson for a telecommunications company selling a new phone system and your target market is midsize companies with a maximum of 150 employees and with sales of $100M or less per year. A typical company this size has a corporate structure that consists of salespeople, engineers, technicians, management, a vice president, a president and a CEO. Typical reasons for the company to change to a new phone system could be increased efficiency over its current cell phone carrier, reduced costs due to the ability to use a broader range of office applications and improved ability to connect with its current IT system, offering an increase in speed of information.

The influencers of a decision to change to the new phone system would be a) a representative from purchasing, due to the reduced costs, b) the IT director, due to his department's increased efficiency and potential reduction of manpower and c) the vice president, who can see the benefit of increased efficiency to the overall company. There will be other potential influencers with less authority, such as salespeople and engineers, but they would not be the ones to elevate and present the concept to the decision makers, who, based on the size of companies you are targeting, would usually be the president and CEO.

Your objective would be to gather information from all the relevant people listed above so that you can identify potential problems for resolution or additional benefits you can offer, which would enable you to justify why the decision maker(s) should meet with you or consider changing to your product.

## Gathering Information and Making Appointments

Sales pros focus on securing appointments and never try to sell their product during the initial call. The quicker you grasp this concept, the more appointments you will make. The object of every new business call is to get an appointment with the decision maker or major influencer without volunteering too much information. Sales pros make appointments their priority and will quickly gather information that they can use to justify the reason for the appointment or utilize to ensure they are prepared for a professional presentation; the average salesperson gives far too much information away and attempts to sell the product during the time he should be developing new business.

Make sure that you read your customer's situation during your call; for example, have you interrupted her? Is she busy? Is she giving off an energy that says "I haven't got time for this"? Most of the time, you will find people in one or more of these states, which means you won't always be given the time to ask all your questions. In such cases, review your list and prioritize your questions so that you ask the important "A" questions first. These will be the questions that quickly uncover the most important information to know if you can justify asking for an appointment. You can then ask the secondary questions during an in-person meeting or a follow-up telephone call.

For example, it would be important to know if this potential customer has just purchased a new competitor's version of what you are selling, or if what you are selling is even needed for her specific industry. If you are a logistics company selling more effective transportation systems, there's little point in taking up her time and yours asking questions if she has just changed over to a new system or if she doesn't ship anything. Asking the right questions can open up an opportunity, eliminate the competition or offer you the chance to expand upon the potential solution you are proposing.

During your initial calls with potential influencers and users, ask questions that identify what they would change or add to their current product if they could, and when you receive an answer, ask why. The idea is to create dissatisfaction for the existing product. You do this by getting someone to talk about the way she presently does something for which you know you have a better solution. Often the more someone talks about a problem, be it big or small, the more dissatisfied she becomes. She may not even think she has a problem until an idea is suggested (by you) that makes her reconsider the situation. What you are doing is focusing her mind; this is another key strategy used by sales pros.

It's imperative to ask questions that relate to how your product affects your prospective customer in relation to her whole operation or situation so that you can fully uncover all needs that your product can meet. Formulate a series of questions, the answers to which enable you to understand what potential solution you can offer that would be of value to your potential customer.

For every question you think of asking, first ask yourself why you are asking it. Redundant questions create confusion and boredom in your potential customer's mind. It's easy to get into a routine of asking questions out of habit without even listening to the answers or remembering to use the answers to offer a reason as to why they should meet with you. The questions you ask become the steering wheel of the conversation, giving you control and direction of the discussion. All sales pros commonly know this as sales drive, which is a trait every sales manager looks for in a sales person.

Prepare by asking yourself: "If I contacted myself and recited my sales pitch, would I give myself an appointment?" If the answer is yes, great, but if the answer is no, retrain and change your approach.

The following questions should be used as a guide to help you have a thorough understanding of how you will position your company and product as you progress toward the opportunity of a presentation and commitment for an order.

1. What are they currently using?

2. How long have they had their existing product?

3. Why did they last change and who made the decision?

4. Who is the main decision maker?

5. Who are the people involved who could influence the decision to move forward?

6. What's their buying process?

7. Who is my competition? (This could be a product user or influencer from within the company you are targeting who has a relationship with the competition.)

8. Why should they listen to me? Why should they give me an appointment?

9. Why should they do something now?

10. Have I sold to similar companies/individuals?

11. What will my challenges be?

12. Do they have the budget?

13. What criteria are important to them?

14. How do I meet the criteria?

15. How do I set the criteria?

16. What will their return on investment be?

## Emotional Triggers

Questions that trigger an emotional connection and response are another focus of the sales pro. You can develop such questions by researching the particular customer's problems. Start by reviewing how your product has helped companies or individuals and identify what results they achieved and what real core problem was eliminated. These core problems were the emotional triggers that enabled the decision maker to move forward. Identifying the emotional reason a person will buy (such as needing greater speed or fear of increased expense) is important.

Define exactly how your product adds value or what it eliminates. Then use that information to emotionally involve the influencer or decision maker you are meeting with. Make a list of all the dissatisfactions your customers could have and identify your solutions. Turn these solutions into questions you can ask your potential customer. Always look at what you could say that would be relevant to his situation and how you could eliminate problems. For example, if you have identified a need for a faster system, you could ask, "What would it mean to you in terms of productivity and financial savings if your current product was 30 percent faster?"

Below are some examples of identifying the emotional trigger and relating that trigger to the results of using your product.

1. Reducing costs relates to a customer's fear of his current costs increasing.

2. Increased speed relates to a customer's need to have a system that improves his capabilities.

3. Improved cash flow relates to a company's desire to increase its buying power by not having too much money tied up.

An additional technique is to turn the results you know your customers want to achieve into closed questions. Asked in a certain way, such questions prompt the person you are talking to into saying yes. For example:

- Are you interested in saving money?
- Could your company benefit from increased cash flow?
- Does increasing the effectiveness of your staff interest you?
- If I could show you a way of reducing your office costs, would you be interested?

The answers to your questions will provide you with the knowledge of how you can potentially help your customer and give you a reason to present to the decision maker as to why he should meet with you.

## The General Benefit Statement

Many times you will find yourself immediately in front of a decision maker before you have had the opportunity to ask questions. In these situations the sales skill used by the sales pro to get an appointment is the general benefit statement.

The general benefit statement is a sentence that incorporates one or two of your product's results. The purpose of this attention-getting statement is to get your customer's attention as quickly as possible. It should create enough interest for a decision maker to want to make an appointment to see you so they can learn more about what you are offering. The more you can define the statement to your potential customer's specific industry, the more powerful it will be.

An attorney, for example, would be interested to know if you have already helped other attorneys track costs and reduce office expenses, thus increasing profitability on each new case. Look at your product and visualize what results your customers or clients are achieving, and then form a sentence that encapsulates those results.

After presenting your statement, always follow up by asking for an appointment. If you sell to business owners and your product has helped other companies save up to 20 percent on their printing costs, your approach could be: "I've recently helped similar companies save up to 20 percent on their printing costs. I'd like to make an appointment to see you next week to discuss whether I could help you do the same."

The following page offers two example phrases that you could use in your approach. Fill in the blank areas with specific customer results achieved for your particular product.

Example 1

Good morning, my name is _____
from _____ and I need to make an appointment
regarding a new _____ that has helped other
successful companies/individuals. [Insert GENERAL BENEFIT
STATEMENT here.] I'm in your area this week and next. Could we
make an appointment on _____, or would _____
be better?

Example 2

Good morning, my name is _____
from _____ and I need to make an appointment
regarding a new _____ that has created a lot
of interest with similar companies/individuals, because [insert
GENERAL BENEFIT STATEMENT here]. I'm in your area this week
and next. Could we make an appointment on _____, or
would _____ be better?

If you encounter an objection, address these concerns using the objection response examples on the following pages and tweak them to make them your own and fit your personality. Remember to be authentic, and practice the responses so you can respond from memory. Always end your response by offering a choice of two days with two different times (for example, Tuesday at 2:15 or Thursday at 10:45). This makes you sound busy and implies the appointment will be brief.

## Objection Response Examples

**Send Me a Brochure**

- "Of course. The brochure is simply a picture of our product, however, and doesn't tell you a great deal about what the product will do for you or your company. We also have several different products that could help to [Insert your General Benefit Statement here], which is why I need to see you in person when I'm in your area talking to other people. It will take only ten or fifteen minutes. Could we make an appointment one day this week?"

**We Are Happy With Our Existing Product**

- "I understand that you're happy with your current product. In fact, most companies now using our product were also happy before hearing what we had to say. I understand you're busy and that's why I'll get straight to the point when we meet. Could we make it for Monday or Wednesday of next week, or would the following week be better?"

**How Much Does It Cost?**

- "Cost is obviously an important factor. Until I have established your exact needs, however, it's not possible to give a firm price. That's why I need to make an appointment to see you one day this week or next."

**We Are Not Interested**

- "I wouldn't expect you to be interested in a product that has not been fully explained. Other customers now using our product responded in the same way. That is the reason for my call. I'm only asking for fifteen minutes one day this week or next. Which would be best for you?"

**We Are Still Not Interested**

- "The reason I persist for an appointment is because we've helped so many other companies similar to yours [Insert your General Benefit Statement here]. They were in the same position as you are now and also hesitant about an appointment, but they're now using our company and benefitting from [Insert your General Benefit Statement here]. The initial appointment only takes twenty minutes. And if we can't help you, then at least you're assured that your current product is the most beneficial for your company. I'm in your area on Monday and Wednesday, or I could make an appointment the following week, if you'd prefer."

**Tell Me Over the Telephone**

- "I appreciate your interest; however, it will take me twenty minutes over the telephone and only five minutes to show you. I am in your area this week and next. Which week is best for you?"

**We Know About It Already**

- "I appreciate that you may have looked before. Could I ask why it was that you did not change? [Use the reason the company did not make the change as the reason to see you for the appointment.] We've just introduced a new product, and other people who also looked before and did not change for the same reasons eventually decided to make the switch once they heard what we had to say. Their reasons, I think, would be of interest to you. Could we make an appointment on Monday or Wednesday, or would the following week be better?"

**I'm Too Busy**

- "I appreciate that you're busy. When we meet, I'll make sure that I get straight to the facts as to why other successful people like you have decided to use our product. I'm in your area this week and next. Could we make an appointment on Monday, or would Wednesday be better?"

**I Really Don't Think We Can Benefit**

- "I appreciate that you're busy and I'm sure our company is the last thing on your mind. We've often been able to ascertain over the telephone or by e-mail whether we can [Insert your General Benefit Statement here]. Could I ask your assistant for some information that will enable me to offer a cost comparison, which I can then forward on to you?"

## Tactics for Getting Past the Gatekeeper

A new business call is effective if you are able to state your case to the correct people. After you've asked questions to gather information from the relevant people, it's time to talk to the decision maker about why and how she would benefit from meeting with you and changing to your product.

But first, you must be able to get beyond the person stopping you from stating your case: the gatekeeper. As a salesperson, it's your job to get the point across properly and to the right person. To make an appointment with someone who cannot make a decision is comparable to an attorney stating the case of his client without a judge or jury present. Always go to the top and be diplomatic along the way, because the assistant or person you are trying to get past could give you inside information and help toward the acceptance of your proposal.

This stage—reaching the decision maker—is crucial for every sales person to master. Once again, your belief in your product's ability to add value—in addition to your charm, creativity and persistence—will determine whether you make it to the next step. Remember, administrative assistants are often well trained on how to screen calls. The objective is to provide only as much information as necessary in order to get through to the person you need to speak with. Adopt the attitude that you require help and explain to the gatekeeper what you're trying to do. You don't want to sound like just another sales call. You want to sound like a person who has something to offer that the decision maker needs.

If you're told the decision maker will call you back, reply, "I'm going to be in and out all day and I'd prefer not to play telephone tag. I'll call back, so could you tell me the best time to do so?"

If you encounter a very persistent gatekeeper, try telephoning early or late when he is not there. Or you could reference the name of your sales manager. Although the gatekeeper would not recognize the name, it creates the perception that perhaps it's a personal friend of the decision maker. For example, "I was referred to Mr. Jones [the decision maker] by [name your sales manager]. Is he available for a moment, please? Thank you." A very authoritative "thank you" will often be all that is needed to get you through.

Another option is to simply appeal to the gatekeeper as an individual. Tell him what you are trying to do and ask for help as to what options he recommends to secure a meeting with the decision maker. Explain that you've helped out many companies similar to theirs and feel you can also offer them a better solution, but that in order to do so, you need to speak to the decision maker.

You could also write a brief e-mail to the decision maker, and personalize it by including the name of the assistant or person within their company whom you spoke to. Reconfirm how you have helped similar companies and include relevant names to personalize it even more. Your e-mail's ending should confirm that, based on your experience with other successful people in a similar industry, you feel he or she could benefit a great deal by a brief meeting. Finish by suggesting two possible appointment dates.

This is a professional approach and should always result in a positive response when you call to confirm the appointment. A similar approach could be used for voicemail; leave a brief message explaining why you need an appointment and suggest a choice of two days when you will be in the area. Confirm that unless you hear differently, you will visit their office to personally provide more details. The fact you said you will visit their office unless you hear from them will trigger a call-back response from the decision maker to ask more questions, confirm an appointment or let you know they are not interested, all of which give you the opportunity to speak with the decision maker to explain why the appointment would be of value. If they don't respond, you have an open door to visit.

## Change Cycle

A change cycle is a period of time a person or company will usually keep a product before a change will be considered. Establishing a change cycle allows you to be more prepared and effective with your time while evaluating potential customers.

Every type of product will normally have a different change cycle. Due to improvements in technology, the time a company spends with any given product has reduced dramatically. You can determine the length of a particular change cycle by asking when the potential customer last changed her existing product, how long she kept the previous one, and, if applicable, how long she had the one before that. After you have this information, work out the average period by adding together the times of all the change cycles and dividing the answer by the total number of products. For example:

### Change Cycle

| | Current Product | Previous Product | Previous Product | Total | Total Divided By # of Products |
|---|---|---|---|---|---|
| First Company | 3 Years | 5 Years | 4 Years | 12 Years | Average 4 Years Per Individual Company |
| Second Company | 4 Years | | | | |
| Third Company | 2.5 Years | | | | |
| Fourth Company | 3.5 Years | | | | |
| Fifth Company | 5 Years | | | | |
| TOTAL | 18 Years | | | | |
| TOTAL Divided By # of Companies | 3.6 Years Industry Average | | | | |

The combined time for the five companies is eighteen years. Divide eighteen by five, and your answer is 3.6; rounding the answer gives an average changing cycle of every 3.5 years. Having established 3.5 years as the change cycle for your product, you know that if the company you are visiting changed its product three years earlier, it's probably going to be ready for a change in about six months.

Identify any possible trend that could affect your equation; for example, the change cycle could have recently increased or decreased. Such trends are opportunities for you to educate your customer, provide the reasoning behind the trend and help her make a better-informed decision about making a switch.

## Customer Call Requests

If you're in the fortunate position to have a potential customer call in to request information (as opposed to you finding her through your new business calls) your first response should be to ask questions that identify what triggered her interest and then schedule an appointment. Such questions include:

How did you get our phone number?

Are you familiar with our company?

What do you currently use?

What are you looking to do differently?

What prompted your call? Why now?

What time frame are you looking at?

What determines your decision?

What is your usual process for making a decision?

Who will make the final decision?

The answers to these questions help you prioritize the appointment in terms of when you visit, whom you see and what your objectives will be. The answers also enable you to have a good understanding of what to expect for the appointment. The more questions you can ask, the clearer the picture will be of what you will need to do to progress the sale.

## Organization, Productivity and Momentum

How you approach each day will be critical to how efficient you are with your time; for example, you may want to target specific areas within your territory or focus on specific industries that you know have a good application for what you are selling. If you have existing accounts, you could organize your day so you blend your existing account calls with new business calls. In addition, events and associations linked to your industry would be good opportunities to network, and attending these would be a useful way to establish yourself as a resource for the company you represent.

One of the many positives for focusing on new business is that when you do find a potential customer, often your competition is not involved. This is because you initiated the conversation. If, on the other hand, the prospective customer makes an inquiry to your company, there is a good chance he has also questioned your competitors. The ability to proactively seek out these potential customers before they realize they need a better solution and start looking for one is a critical part of the sales process and separates the sales pro from the average sales performer.

Before you start your new business activities each day, organize your tasks and goals so that you can get the most out of your time. Most salespeople use computers or iPads to organize and increase their effectiveness and you'll find many software applications available to help you. Focus on the next day's appointments the night before, ensure you have telephone numbers in case you're going to be late, and list backup activities you can accomplish should an appointment cancel or you have additional time on your hands. Write down what you are going to say and a couple of answers to certain objections you may get. Having a sample script for reference will give you more confidence. When you prepare beforehand, there is time to strategically think about what you are going to do and say.

New business development should always be consistent, so make sure you set aside a certain amount of time every day, week or month. Successful salespeople don't set aside time for a while and then stop; it's a discipline. Maintaining momentum is a key component to good business development. Analyze your own activity and ask yourself: What more could I be doing? Am I being effective at this moment? If you ask yourself this at least four times a day, and if you make the necessary changes, you will stay motivated and your results will change dramatically. You'll gradually see where you've been wasting your time. Make a point of making an early call and a late call each day; you are more likely to work harder between those calls, and not start late or finish early.

Always finish what you start, even if you hear that another salesperson has just prospected where you are or made telephone contact with the person you have just called; their activity may have created a platform of interest that you can leverage. Never prejudge or assume the potential customer has no need, and keep moving forward until you have achieved the goal or objective you have set for yourself. Have a realistic objective for what you want to accomplish in addition to securing an appointment, such as gathering information on what the customer is currently using, how long he has had it, who the decision makers and influencers are or if the company owns or leases what it is currently using. Set yourself a daily or weekly goal, as this will increase your sense of urgency to achieve your objectives.

## Open Field

As you win sales and start to transition towards your sales pro status, you will benefit tremendously during your new business development activities by focusing on the success of past results. If you are selling to companies, review past successes to gain a better understanding of specific industries, such as healthcare, education, government or commercial. If you are selling to individuals, identify potential trends that could show where you are having more success. For example, you could be having more success with men instead of women, older people instead of younger or families instead of individuals. This knowledge will increase your confidence, offer you a more defined target and may yield discoveries of new potential customers.

Establish activities that yield good results, and focus on finding leads by pursuing those activities. With each activity, establish how much you need to do to achieve the results you have set for yourself. For example, if you've established that five activities such as networking, physical prospecting, direct mail, trade shows and telephone prospecting can generate an appointment, but you hate two of them, then work on the three you like and establish how much activity you need to do to achieve the desired result. The key is to work on the activities you like and not the ones you don't.

Remember, there is someone out there who has a tremendous need for your product. If you don't get to them, however, they'll never know what they're missing.

# PROSPECTING

## CARTOON STORY

HI, MARIE, I LEARNED SOME MORE INFORMATION ABOUT PROSPECTING FROM MY WORKBOOK TODAY.

WHAT WAS THAT, PETE?

WELL, FIRST, ONCE YOU HAVE BEEN SELLING FOR A FEW MONTHS, LOOK BACK TO THE SALES YOU HAVE MADE AND SEE WHAT INDUSTRY OR TYPE OF INDIVIDUALS YOU HAVE MAINLY BEEN SUCCESSFUL WITH.

OH I KNOW, THEN PHONE THOSE TYPES OF INDIVIDUALS OR COMPANIES.

EXACTLY. YOU CAN ALSO TAKE ADVANTAGE OF YOUR PAST SALES TO THOSE TYPES OF INDIVIDUALS OR COMPANIES BY SAYING THAT YOU HAVE GENUINELY HELPED OUT OTHER SUCCESSFUL INDIVIDUALS OR COMPANIES SIMILAR TO THEM, AND THAT'S WHY YOU NEED TO SEE THEM SO YOU CAN SHOW THEM HOW OTHER COMPANIES ARE BENEFITTING FROM YOUR PRODUCT OR SERVICE.

I'VE BEEN USING THAT FOR A WHILE NOW, AND IT HAS REALLY HELPED ME INCREASE MY APPOINTMENTS FROM THE SAME NUMBER OF CALLS. I'VE ALSO HAD GREAT SUCCESS FROM REFERRAL PROSPECTING—HAVE YOU TRIED IT YET?

I HAVEN'T HAD TIME TO. I'M STILL ON MY SALES COURSE, BUT ONCE I'VE FINISHED I'M GOING TO CALL ALL MY PAST CUSTOMERS AND ASK FOR AT LEAST ONE REFERRAL FROM EACH. ALTHOUGH I HAVEN'T MANY CUSTOMERS YET, I'M GOING TO MAKE FULL USE OF THE ONES I HAVE!

EXCELLENT, BUT REMEMBER TO HELP THEM WHEN YOU CALL BY NARROWING IT DOWN, FOR EXAMPLE, TO A PARTICULAR BUSINESS GROUP OR CLUB THEY MAY BELONG TO. IF YOU JUST ASK IF THEY KNOW OF ANYONE ELSE THAT COULD ALSO BENEFIT FROM YOUR SERVICE, YOU'RE PROBABLY GOING TO GET A LONG PAUSE OR BLANK STARE BECAUSE YOU'RE ASKING TOO BROAD A QUESTION. SO REMEMBER TO KEEP IT EASY FOR THEM.

YES, I SEE. MAKE IT EASY FOR THEM TO THINK OF OTHER BUSINESS PEOPLE THEY ASSOCIATE WITH. THAT WAY YOU'RE GETTING THEM TO FOCUS ON A SPECIFIC GROUP OF PEOPLE AND NOT EVERYONE. I ALSO KNOW THAT JOHN'S APPROACH IS TO SAY "I'M NOT ASKING YOU TO REFER ME TO PEOPLE YOU KNOW WILL NEED OUR SERVICE. ONLY TO PEOPLE WHO WOULD LET ME INTRODUCE OUR COMPANY BASED ON THE STRENGTH OF YOUR RECOMMENDATION."

WHAT ELSE HAVE YOU LEARNED?

THAT IT'S IMPORTANT TO BE DISCIPLINED AND CONSISTENT WITH YOUR NEW CALLS, AND TO ALWAYS FINISH WHAT YOU START. ALSO TO SET YOURSELF AN OBJECTIVE OF SO MANY CALLS OR HOURS OF PROSPECTING, AND NOT STOPPING UNTIL YOU HAVE REACHED THAT OBJECTIVE.

THAT'S RIGHT, I REMEMBER I USED TO START MAKING CALLS FROM A LIST AND AFTER THE FIRST TEN OR TWENTY CALLS I WOULD GET A BAD FEELING SO I WOULD CHANGE TO A DIFFERENT LIST, AND THEN ANOTHER, MAINLY BECAUSE I WAS GETTING A BAD REACTION FROM THE PEOPLE I WAS CALLING, LIKE "WE'VE JUST HAD SOMEONE CALL US ABOUT THAT LAST WEEK," OR "YOU'RE THE FIFTH PERSON TODAY TO CALL."

YES, THAT HAPPENED TO ME. NOW I KNOW WHY OUR TOP SALES PERSON FINISHES ALL THE CALLS ON THE LISTS THAT HAVE ONLY BEEN HALF CALLED. HE SEES THEM ALL AS OPPORTUNITIES REGARDLESS OF WHAT REACTION HE IS GETTING. HE KEEPS GOING UNTIL HE FINISHES HIS LIST AND OTHERS THAT ARE LYING AROUND.

I ALSO LEARNED THAT ONCE YOU WORK OUT YOUR CONVERSION RATE OF HOW MANY CALLS YOU NORMALLY MAKE TO GET AN APPOINTMENT, YOU CAN SEE THAT EACH NEW CALL YOU MAKE IS LIKE PICKING UP MONEY. ALL YOU DO IS DIVIDE THE TOTAL NUMBER OF CALLS IT TAKES YOU TO GET A SALE BY YOUR AVERAGE COMMISSION FOR EACH SALE.

THAT'S RIGHT - IT MEANS EVEN WHEN YOU GET A "NO" YOU CAN SAY THAT YOU EARNED MONEY JUST FOR MAKING THE CALL. AND OF COURSE, THE MORE "NO'S" YOU GET, THE NEARER YOU ARE TO A "YES."

YOU'RE RIGHT, IF IT TAKES TWENTY CALLS TO GET AN APPOINTMENT AND YOU HAVE ESTABLISHED THAT YOU GET ONE SALE FOR EVERY FOUR APPOINTMENTS, THEN YOU KNOW THAT YOU NORMALLY HAVE TO MAKE EIGHTY CALLS TO MAKE A SALE. THEN IF YOUR AVERAGE SALE IS $5000 AND YOU GET 10% COMMISSION, YOU WOULD KNOW THAT FOR EVERY NEW CALL YOU MAKE, THEY HAND YOU $6.25.

WE SHOULD ALWAYS BE LEARNING, SHOULDN'T WE? AFTER ALL, WHEN YOU THINK ABOUT IT, IF YOU FINISH WHAT YOU START, YOU FEEL MUCH BETTER THAN DOING SOMETHING ONLY HALF WAY THROUGH, AND REALLY WE SHOULD LOOK AT THE TOP PEOPLE AND SEE WHAT IS WORKING FOR THEM. IF WE HAD DONE THAT WE WOULD HAVE LEARNED THIS A LOT SOONER.

HOW ABOUT MIXING YOUR PROSPECTING. DO YOU KNOW ABOUT THAT?

YES, I LEARNED ALL ABOUT THAT FROM THE WORKBOOK WHEN I WAS LOOKING THROUGH TO FIND OUT HOW TO CALCULATE MY CONVERSIONS OF NEW CALLS AND APPOINTMENTS AND AVERAGE ORDER VALUES. MIXING MY PROSPECTING WILL REALLY HELP BECAUSE I'VE ALWAYS PROSPECTED IN ONE DIRECTION, WHICH IS ON THE TELEPHONE. NOW I'M GOING TO MAKE PHYSICAL CALLS, REFERRAL CALLS, AND NETWORKING CALLS TOO!

AND WHEN I REALLY GET GOING, IN ABOUT SIX MONTHS, I'M GOING TO GET MY OWN TELEMARKETER TO ALSO PHONE FOR ME.

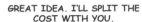

GREAT IDEA. I'LL SPLIT THE COST WITH YOU.

GREAT! ANOTHER POINT I LEARNED THAT I DIDN'T APPRECIATE BEFORE WAS THAT PART OF THE MOTIVATION WHEN YOU'RE PROSPECTING IS THAT WHEN YOU DO GET AN APPOINTMENT, YOU ARE NORMALLY THE ONLY COMPANY INVOLVED IN PROPOSING YOUR TYPE OF PRODUCT, SO YOU HAVE A GOOD CHANCE OF SELLING WITHOUT THE COMPETITION GETTING INVOLVED.

YES, I'VE FOUND THAT WHEN I DO GET A LEAD FROM SOMEONE WHO HAS CALLED IN, THEY'VE OFTEN ALSO CALLED THREE OR FOUR OTHER COMPANIES TOO. ALTHOUGH MY WORKBOOK HAS TAUGHT ME HOW TO SELL AGAINST COMPETITION, IT'S OBVIOUSLY MUCH BETTER IF THEY AREN'T PART OF THE PICTURE.

WELL, I'VE GOT SOME TIME TO MAKE A FEW NEW CALLS. COMING?

SURE, AND I'LL BET YOU $10 THAT I MAKE THREE APPOINTMENTS BEFORE YOU DO!

YOU'RE ON!

# SEVEN

# The Winning Presentation Formula

The sole purpose of the presentation is to prove what you have previously proposed. The information that you gathered from the questions asked at the time of making the appointment, or subsequent time afterwards, should have helped you determine which products you are going to present, what differentiation you have identified, what additional benefits match the needs of your customer and to whom you need to present them.

One of the most common mistakes sales people make is to present their product solution to people who are not the decision makers or to only some of the decision makers. Prevent these situations by making sure you have all the decision makers in front of you before starting the presentation, or at least by confirming that you will be able to present to any additional decision makers or influencers in a follow-up meeting.

## Instill Confidence

Before you enter into your presentation, it is imperative that you present evidence of your ability to respond to the customer's needs and provide the additional ongoing service and support that will be required after the sale is completed. Often a person making a decision is nervous or unsure of whether the decision she is about to make is the right one. She needs to feel secure and confident that her decision is not going to blow up in her face. Changing from one company or product to another entails risk on her part. The unknown is a good-enough reason to stay with the brand she currently has, and it's your job to either reinforce that brand (if the brand is yours) or refocus her on how the brand you are selling is more advantageous and entails zero risk.

An important consideration is that the customer's psychological reaction will be different when something goes wrong with a purchase from a new brand compared to the same error with a familiar brand. For example, a person may be used to a certain brand of car. If he renews his lease with the same car brand but something goes wrong with the new car, he just gets it repaired and drives off again; his initial focus isn't on worrying about the quality of the brand of car. If he changes his car brand, however, and then something goes wrong, he will likely feel that choosing the new brand was the wrong decision after all.

The same type of situation occurs in an office environment. If the malfunctioning new machine is the same brand the company has been using, the focus is on repairing the new machine. But if the decision was made to switch brands and the machine starts malfunctioning, all eyes are on the person who made the "crazy" decision to change.

This is an important concept for all sales people to remember. Put yourself in the position of the decision maker and make her feel confident and secure in doing business with you.

## Pre-Presentation

The sales pro always presents evidence of his ability to respond to the needs of his customer, instilling the trust needed to make a decision, before he leads into his actual presentation. He accomplishes this during his initial appointment with a brief pre-presentation of his company and its product, existing customer information, testimonials, highlights of the specific product he is going to present and the potential results the customer can expect. If his initial appointment is at the same time as his actual presentation, the presentation would naturally follow the pre-presentation. Every sales person should ensure he has captured the pertinent information about his product and prepared his pre-presentation so he, too, can immediately create a credible platform from which to move forward.

Your pre-presentation could be in the form of a PowerPoint from your computer or tablet or printed out and put into a three-ring binder. Structure all the pages based on the sequence below, with the information on each page shown as bullet points. Keep the information simple. You will need to create several options for pages five and six, as these relate to the specific product solution you are going to present, which may change depending on the needs of each potential customer.

As you talk through each of the six pages, make sure you are interacting with your customer, asking questions about each aspect of the presentation and listening and responding to her answers.

## PowerPoint Slide Examples

The answers from your questions to pages one and two will offer you good information on your customer's knowledge of your company and products.

The notes within the PowerPoint slides below will offer you sample questions to ask your customer for each slide.

These six pages reinforce your professionalism and make your prospective customer feel confident, and will increase his security in the knowledge that forming a business relationship between his company and yours would not be a mistake.

## PowerPoint Slide Notes

### Page 1
#### Introduction of Your Company

**Notes:** "Mr. Jones, thank you for the opportunity to meet and discuss how we may be able to help provide a solution for your company. Before I start, can I ask if you have ever heard of our company before?"

– Listen and respond to his answer, and if the answer is no, present the bullet points outlined on the page. Once you've finished, ask if he has any questions.

### Page 2
#### Overview of Your Products

**Notes:** "Mr. Jones, we represent the XYZ product. Are you familiar with that?"

– Listen and respond to his answer, and if the answer is no, present the bullet points on the page.

### Page 3
#### List of Your Local or National Accounts

**Notes:** "Mr. Jones, due to our company and product strengths, we have been able to secure long-term relationships with some of the major local and national accounts. Are you familiar with any of these?"

### Page 4
#### Testimonial Highlights from Existing Customers

**Notes:** "This is what a few of our customers have said regarding the results they have been able to achieve."

### Page 5
#### Specific Product Details

(Customize to the Product Solution You Have Identified)

**Notes:** "Mr. Jones, after reviewing your needs, this is the product I will be presenting to you."

### Page 6
#### The General Benefit Statement

(Results Achieved by the Specific Product)

**Notes:** "And these are the results you would be able to achieve."

After presenting your final page, follow up with, "Before I present our product, do you have any questions?"

# PRE-PRESENTATION

## CARTOON STORY

WELL, FIRST, WHEN I ARRIVE, I RECONFIRM IF ANYONE ELSE NEEDS TO BE PRESENT FOR THE DECISION MAKING OR USAGE OF THE SYSTEM.

ISN'T THAT OBVIOUS? AFTER ALL, IF THEY MADE THE APPOINTMENT, SURELY THEY CAN MAKE A DECISION.

NOT ALWAYS. IN FACT, I HAVE OFTEN USED UP ALL MY ENERGY WITH AN ENTHUSIASTIC, HIGH-POWERED, AND FLAWLESS PRESENTATION ONLY TO FIND OUT THAT ANOTHER DECISION MAKER NEEDED TO BE PRESENT. FROM THE START, THE CUSTOMER I HAD PRESENTED TO HAD "AN OBJECTION THAT STANDS UP IN COURT."

AN OBJECTION THAT STANDS UP IN COURT?

YES, AN OBJECTION THAT CANNOT BE OVERCOME. AFTER ALL, HOW CAN MY CUSTOMER MAKE A DECISION WITHOUT THEIR BUSINESS PARTNER OR SPOUSE THERE?

ABSOLUTELY, THAT'S WHY YOU HEAR TOP SALESPEOPLE SAYING, "POOR SELLING CREATES OBJECTIONS." SO IF THERE IS SOMEONE ELSE WHO SHOULD BE THERE, YOU'RE BEST OFF TO RESCHEDULE. HOWEVER, IF YOU HAVE ALL THE DECISION MAKERS THERE, THEN I WOULD LEAVE MY PRODUCT IN ITS CASE AND START BY GOING BACK OVER THE INFORMATION I HAD GATHERED PREVIOUSLY WITH THE CUSTOMER.

I SEE, FINDING YOURSELF IN THAT SITUATION CAN BE COMPARED TO A LAWYER IN COURT WITHOUT A JUDGE. YOU REALLY HAVE CREATED YOUR OWN CONDITION FROM THE START, HAVEN'T YOU.

I SEE... THAT WAY YOU'RE RE-EDUCATING THEM ABOUT THEIR PRESENT PRODUCT AND PROBLEMS.

YOU'VE GOT IT. THEN IF I FORGET TO ASK ANY QUESTIONS THAT COULD BE RELEVANT I WOULD ASK THEM AT THIS STAGE. THEN I WOULD FOLLOW WITH A SMALL INTRODUCTION OF OUR COMPANY AND CLIENT LIST, TOGETHER WITH DETAILS OF WHAT WE HAVE ACHIEVED TO DATE AND WHAT OUR MISSION IS.

I NEVER THOUGHT OF THAT. NORMALLY I JUST GET MY PRODUCT OUT AND LEAD INTO MY PRESENTATION AS QUICKLY AS POSSIBLE, BUT I CAN SEE HOW THAT DOESN'T LOOK VERY PROFESSIONAL.

EXACTLY! ALSO YOUR CUSTOMER MAY HAVE FORGOTTEN WHAT YOU HAD TALKED ABOUT PREVIOUSLY, OR HAVE OTHER THINGS ON THEIR MIND.

I SEE THAT NOW. SO WOULD YOU NOW GET OUT YOUR PRODUCT AND START PRESENTING?

NO, AFTER I HAD ASKED IF ANYONE ELSE WOULD BE ATTENDING, THEN INTRODUCED OUR COMPANY AND CLIENT LIST, I WOULD RECAP WHAT WE HAD DISCUSSED PREVIOUSLY, REFLECT BACK THEIR CURRENT PROBLEM AREAS THAT WE HAD ESTABLISHED COULD BE IMPROVED AND THEN GET A COMMITMENT. IF I COULD OFFER A SOLUTION, THEY WOULD BE INTERESTED, WOULDN'T THEY?

SO THEN WOULD YOU LEAD INTO THE PRESENTATION?

YES, AND ONLY THEN. NORMALLY IT TAKES ABOUT 15 MINUTES, BUT IT'S THE MOST IMPORTANT 15 MINUTES YOU COULD SPEND WITH YOUR CUSTOMER. I'VE HAD CUSTOMERS SAY HOW PROFESSIONAL MY APPROACH IS AND HOW THEY FEEL AS THOUGH I AM REALLY TRYING TO HELP THEM AND THEIR BUSINESS.

## The Actual Presentation

It's time for the actual presentation. Your presentation should reinforce what you have already said your customer will gain by owning or using your product. In the mind of the sales pro, she already has the sale completed before the presentation. She has the trust of her customer and has reinforced in previous meetings the potential value to be gained.

Now she simply needs to reinforce the facts to ensure the sale. This is where the time you have spent researching your competition, fully knowing your product and identifying everything there is to know about your customer's current product, the criteria important to him and his buying process will pay off.

## Connecting with Your Presentation

Whether you have to jump up and down, scream in your car or run around in circles before your presentation to increase your energy level, make sure you portray an authentic enthusiasm that ignites your audience. I've seen too many average salespeople present their product with a lack of excitement that only reinforces that it's time for them to move on and find something they really are excited about. How can a customer be excited and enthusiastic if the salesperson isn't? Enthusiasm makes your presentation exciting and enjoyable for both you and your prospective customer, adding the extra sparkle to everything you say. Without it, your presentation will be lifeless and boring. Prospective customers will become distracted and unfocused.

Enthusiasm is born out of the absolute belief that what you are about to present is the best option for your potential customer. Energize your presentation by focusing on your belief in the results he will achieve by using your product. This energy and conviction will ensure success and increase your sales. Smile and speak as though you are in your prospective customer's position and are about to make a big decision, one that will have only a positive impact on him and his business. Constantly remind yourself of the last four letters of enthusiasm: I.A.S.M. Turn this into your new motto: "I am sold myself."

## Customize to Your Customer

Most sales companies will have a written script that reinforces what to say and when to say it while presenting their product. Although this is important to learn and utilize as your initial structure for the presentation, the difference between the average sales performer evolving into a sales pro is his ability to tailor the presentation to the customer. The sales pro tailors every presentation to each individual customer. He uses the answers from his questions to create the flow of the presentation so that it becomes a customized, interactive experience.

Too many salespeople ask questions at the start and then don't use the information they have obtained during the presentation. They ask a few questions, totally ignore the answers they receive and get straight into the presentation without mentioning how their product will benefit the customer. They are too eager to show how good they are at presenting their "textbook" presentation, when in fact they end up ignoring and boring the customer. Don't make the mistake of focusing on what you are presenting at the expense of what's important to your audience.

Make sure to include the solutions to the customer's problems as you are presenting, as well as creating dissatisfaction for the product he is currently using. You create dissatisfaction by focusing your questions on a specific feature you know his current product doesn't have but that he could benefit from, getting him to talk about the problems he is experiencing by not having it and asking him what the payoff would be if he did.

The first step in being able to achieve customization is to commit to memory any script you may have been given so that the information becomes natural, authentic and molded to your personality. This is an important step in the presentation process and can only be accomplished by investing the time to fully comprehend the information. It will require rehearsing the presentation over and over again, just like an actor rehearsing his lines.

# PRESENTATION

CARTOON STORY

I WASN'T USING THE ANSWERS TO MY INITIAL QUESTIONS DURING MY PRESENTATION.

WHAT'S WRONG WITH THAT?

THAT'S THE POINT. THE IDEA IS TO REMIND THEM OF HOW THEY ARE CURRENTLY DOING IT EVERY TIME YOU GET TO A BENEFIT OF YOUR PRODUCT IN YOUR PRESENTATION.

I NEVER THOUGHT OF THAT BEFORE. I JUST ASSUMED THEY WOULD SEE HOW MY PRODUCT OR SERVICE WOULD BENEFIT THEM COMPARED TO THEIR EXISTING SYSTEM DURING MY PRESENTATION.

SO YOU REMIND THEM EVERY TIME YOU GET TO A BENEFIT OF HOW THAT PARTICULAR BENEFIT WILL BE OF USE COMPARED TO WHAT THEY ARE PRESENTLY DOING.

SO THEY DON'T SEE IT AS JUST A PRESENTATION YOU GIVE TO EVERYONE.

EXACTLY! THAT WAY THE PRESENTATION IS ALWAYS SHOWING THEM HOW THEY WILL BENEFIT AGAINST WHAT THEY ARE CURRENTLY USING.

YES, THAT'S RIGHT. YOU SEE, IF YOU JUST LEAD INTO YOUR PRESENTATION, THEN YOU'RE TELLING AND NOT SELLING!

YES, PLUS YOU'RE NOT MAKING IT INTERESTING FOR THEM!

## Presentation Platform

The structure of your overall presentation, including how you customize the material and create the platform that reinforces your credibility before you even lead into your presentation, is important because it must cover all the details relevant to the decision makers and those who can influence the decision.

If you are in the position of selling a product where the actual presentation occurs at the same time as the initial call, then your presentation platform would have already been covered by your pre-presentation, and you can go straight to the eight presentation steps. Before you start your presentation, however, make sure the decision maker and major influencers are present.

1) **Formalities** – Keep initial conversation brief, reestablishing rapport.

2) **Decision-Maker Confirmation** – Confirm all decision makers and people who will influence the decision are present. This ensures a decision can be made at the time of the presentation.

3) **Company and Product Reintroduction** – Remind your audience who you represent and what product you are going to present.

4) **Situation Review** – Recap the original information you gathered from your initial questions.

5) **General Benefit Statement** – Present your general benefit statement to confirm the results they will receive from your product.

6) **Transition** – Lead into the presentation and prove what you have proposed.

## Eight-Step Presentation

As you transition through each step, make sure you continually equate the differences between the customer's current product or system and what you are proposing.

1) **Matching Benefits** – Specify benefits that match the needs of your customer.

2) **Raising the Perception** – Increase the importance of a matching benefit.

3) **Testing the Water** – Check for customer commitment.

4) **Involving the Senses** – Focus your communication to auditory, kinesthetic and visual aspects and learners.

5) **Emotional Connection** – Connect to the heart in addition to the head.

6) **Price Presentation** – Justify the financial investment.

7) **Reason to Buy Today** – Create a sense of urgency.

8) **Close** – Assume the commitment.

# 1) Matching Benefits

The sales pro focuses on matching benefits, which are those benefits of your product that you have established will be of prime interest to your prospective customer. Matching benefits are not necessarily *unique* benefits or differentiators but the benefits of your product that match what your customers are looking for. Of course, there will be times when a specific matching benefit will also offer differentiation and in such cases the impact to your customer will be even greater. Establish matching benefits by reviewing the information you gathered during your initial questioning and work out which features—and, in turn, which benefits—will be of value to your customer.

The average-performing salesperson doesn't always think about how what she is presenting matches the information she may have been told by her customer, and she will usually only talk about benefits of her product that she herself likes, or she simply makes a list of all the benefits that her product offers, memorizes them, and then spills them out to every prospective customer she can. Since she doesn't think about which benefits, if any, the prospective customer is interested in, she hopes that by presenting all of them, the prospective customer will be dazzled and buy. This is, in fact, *telling* and not *selling*. By talking about all the benefits, the important matching benefits the customer is really interested in will be diluted.

Can you **see** how you are immediately drawn to the words that **stand** out? The words that have been highlighted can be compared with matching benefits. Look at the un-highlighted words and see how they merge into the text. If not highlighted, the importance and **power** of your matching benefits will be **diluted** by all the other benefits.

Your ability to properly introduce a matching benefit at the right time increases your potential customer's appreciation of it and helps progress the sale. Ensure you have questioned him enough on the specific problem the matching benefit resolves before you present it as a solution. Volunteering information too early is a natural trait of the average sales person. The excitement of identifying a benefit they know matches what their customer is looking for makes them want to tell their customer as soon as possible. Never make the mistake of volunteering information too early.

# MATCHING BENEFITS

## CARTOON STORY

## 2) Raising the Perception

Before the sales pro presents a matching benefit, they get the customer to talk about that particular area of concern or existing way of doing something. This creates dissatisfaction for their existing system and increases their desire for a solution. If you're not raising the perception of a benefit before offering it, you are dramatically reducing the impact it will have on your potential customer.

Here's how it works: Before offering the first matching benefit, raise the perception of it by getting the customer to talk about the particular concern associated with not having a solution. Once they have referred to their problems or existing way of doing something, ask how much it is costing in time, money or productivity by not having the solution. Listen and respond and then follow with the presentation of the matching benefit. The impact of presenting your matching benefits this way can be tremendous, because by reintroducing the question before highlighting the matching benefit, you are increasing the need and desire for a solution.

Consider the following example, in which you are selling a car that has a central locking device, which you know from your questions that your customer needs but is not aware of.

| | |
|---|---|
| SALES PRO: | "Mr. Jones, I understand your existing car requires all the doors to be locked separately." |
| CUSTOMER: | "Yes, that's correct." |
| SALES PRO: | "How do you confirm all the doors are locked?" |
| CUSTOMER: | "We have to physically check each door before we leave the car." |
| SALES PRO: | "Mr. Jones, how important is security to you? Have you ever accidently left a door unlocked?" |
| CUSTOMER: | "Absolutely. In fact, we had some items stolen a few months ago, so now I double-check each door." |
| SALES PRO: | "How did that affect you? Did the insurance cover you?" |
| CUSTOMER: | "My insurance didn't cover the loss because the car wasn't fully locked." |

SALES PRO: "How advantageous would it be if, when you locked your driver door, all the doors locked?"

CUSTOMER: "It would be a tremendous advantage. I wouldn't have to worry all the time."

By reminding the customer of the situation that occurred, the sales pro raised the perception in the customer's mind of a need for a solution. Without a central locking feature, theft could occur again; thus, the sales pro immediately enhanced the customer's desire to find a solution.

You can see how this presentation becomes much more effective than if the salesperson had simply said, "Mr. Jones, this car has a central locking feature." The latter approach is not using each benefit to its fullest advantage, and is known as telling and not selling

It may appear as if you are stating the obvious, and in fact you are, but good communication is a reinforcement of the obvious, allowing everyone to be on the same page.

Raising the perception in your customer's mind this way magnifies the need for a solution. This technique also eliminates the possibility of your assuming something you shouldn't. Always remember the power of your benefits. You can use them to confirm the sale, or to open the sale for someone else.

# RAISING THE PERCEPTION

## CARTOON STORY

WELL, BEFORE SHOWING THEM THE SOLUTION I WOULD FIRST ASK THEM ABOUT THE PROBLEM AND HOW THEY WERE PRESENTLY COPING.

SO YOU WOULD START OFF WITH A QUESTION.

YES, THAT WAY THEY HAVE TO ANSWER ME. WHICH MEANS THAT ANYTHING ELSE THAT IS ON THEIR MIND HAS TO TAKE SECOND PLACE.

SO THEY EXPLAIN TO YOU HOW THEY ARE HANDLING THEIR CURRENT PROBLEM AREA.

YES, ALTHOUGH THEY MAY NOT EVEN KNOW IT'S A PROBLEM UNTIL I RECONFIRM WHAT PROBLEMS WERE BEING CAUSED AS A RESULT OF DOING IT THEIR CURRENT WAY.

HOW WOULD YOU KNOW THAT?

BECAUSE I WOULD HAVE ALREADY ESTABLISHED ON MY INITIAL CALL WHAT THEY WERE PRESENTLY DOING AND HOW IT WAS CAUSING PROBLEMS AND HOW WHAT I COULD OFFER WOULD ELIMINATE THOSE PROBLEMS.

BUT WHAT IF THEY DIDN'T KNOW THEY HAD A PROBLEM? OH, I SEE, THAT'S WHY YOU GET THEM TO TALK ABOUT IT SO THEY REALIZE THERE COULD BE A BETTER WAY OF DOING IT. WHAT YOU'RE DOING IS CREATING A DISSATISFACTION SO YOU CAN OFFER A SOLUTION.

YOU'VE GOT IT! THE MORE THEY TALK ABOUT IT, THE MORE I AM RAISING THE PERCEPTION OF THE VALUE OF THE BENEFIT I AM ABOUT TO OFFER. THE BENEFIT BECOMES THEIR SOLUTION.
HOWEVER, BEFORE SHOWING THEM THE BENEFIT I WOULD PRE-CONFIRM THAT IF A BENEFIT WERE OFFERED THEY WOULD BE INTERESTED.

## 3) Testing the Water

Test closing is another term for testing the water within the presentation. It means asking a question that does not confirm the sale, but confirms your customer's potential commitment level. For example, you could walk into a home or office with your product and say, "Where will you be using the product? I can set it up." This question invites a response that subconsciously creates acceptance of your product. This is a better approach than walking in and saying, "Shall I set it up over here?"

As you go through your presentation, you raise the perception of the first matching benefit you are about to present. You then present the matching benefit, explain how the benefit offers the solution, and then test the water by asking, "Can you see how that will help?" or "Do you agree that this benefit will save time and reduce costs against your existing product?"

Once you get a positive response to your testing-the-water question, continue your presentation by offering another matching benefit and repeat the testing process. This method of testing the water by getting agreement from your prospective customer makes your customer gradually feel more and more comfortable to commit to move forward with the product you are presenting, because they've been giving positive responses all the way through.

The more confirmations you can get, the better your chance of progressing the sale. Test closing is all about getting positive feedback so that you can continue along your path toward the order being signed. Sales pros test the water throughout their presentation, getting feedback from their prospective customer, which confirms whether their presentation is going in the right direction. If they get a negative response or a question, they can stop, answer and continue, or redirect the presentation as necessary. Sales pros use this technique as a way of asking themselves whether they're still on course.

The bouncing bomb, invented during World War II, relates well to testing the water. The bomber pilots could not fly near enough to a major dam they needed to eliminate, so the bouncing bomb was invented. The idea was to fly the bomber low to the water, keep it absolutely level, and drop a bomb that, on contact with the water, would bounce forward off the water surface toward the dam.

## 5) Emotional Connection

Emotion opens up the sale and logic shuts it tight. People start off buying emotionally: "I would love one!" Or logically: "I need one!" Ask yourself, "Why do I buy?" Pride, fear, profit, love and need are a few of the emotional reasons that will subconsciously motivate customers to buy. If you haven't incorporated their emotional reason for buying and then ask for the order but don't receive confirmation, it's often because you didn't open them up emotionally.

Tapping into a prospective customer's emotions is an important skill to master, as it allows you to speak to a different part of their brain. The brain naturally opens up when emotion is involved and enhances the connection to the information being given. Therefore, while presenting your product, note both the customer's emotional response and his logical response to what you are saying.

You may have a customer who loves the product you are selling. He gets enjoyment in just owning more of what he loves. Or you could have someone who has an immediate need because his old product is broken, or perhaps someone already has an old product of yours that he feels could break down any minute, so his motivation for buying is based on fear of being left without. You could have a customer who will profit immediately by having what you are offering, especially if your product offers something like a lower interest rate, or better fuel economy. Finally, you could have someone who is very image-conscious and who takes pride in owning the newest and the best.

The idea is to present your product and incorporate the potential customer's emotional reason for buying. You do this by reconfirming his emotional reason for buying throughout the presentation. This will give your presentation warmth and pull your potential customer toward buying from you. For example, if your prospective customer's major motivation for buying is pride and profit, and you don't persist on these two aspects of your product, or if you persist in pushing two different areas such as fear and need, your presentation will be as cold as ice because you have missed the customer's emotional connection to your product.

On the other hand, if you only persist on his one or two emotional motivators but do not present the gains he'll receive, you'll have opened him up emotionally but have yet to shut down the sale logically. This is why all areas of your presentation are important. You have to use everything you can. Be prepared to spend the time it takes, and ask or redirect questions until you get all the information you need to progress or confirm the sale.

# EMOTIONAL CONNECTION

## CARTOON STORY

SO HOW DO YOU FIND YOUR *CUSTOMER'S* EMOTIONAL REASONS FOR BUYING?

WELL, FIRST BY LOOKING AROUND THEIR OFFICE. WHAT YOU SEE COULD SHOW YOU THAT THEY ENJOY QUALITY, OR ONLY BUY WHAT THEY NEED, OR LIKE GADGETS. THEY MAY BE IMAGE-CONSCIOUS BASED ON THE WAY THEY DRESS OR THE CAR THEY DRIVE.

I SEE. WHAT YOU'RE ALSO ESTABLISHING IS THEIR BUYING STYLE. YOU ALSO NEED TO ASK QUESTIONS AND LISTEN CAREFULLY TO ANSWERS.

YES, THEY MIGHT SAY "I NEED TO *CHANGE*," OR ASK "WHAT IF IT BREAKS DOWN?"

RIGHT, SO IN THOSE SITUATIONS YOU HAVE NEED, PRIDE AND FEAR.

OKAY, SO YOU WOULD BE DOING THIS WHILE YOU'RE GATHERING INFORMATION, MATCHING BENEFITS, SHOWING THEM THE PRODUCT OR SERVICE, AND GIVING THEM A REASON TO BUY TODAY!

EXACTLY, SO THEN YOU HIGHLIGHT OTHER AREAS OF YOUR PRODUCT OR SERVICE THAT ALSO COULD FALL INTO THE SAME CATEGORY.

VERY GOOD! THAT'S EXACTLY HOW IT WORKS. IF YOU HAVEN'T ESTABLISHED AN EMOTIONAL REASON TO BUY, YOU END UP WITH A COLD PRESENTATION.

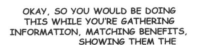

## 6) Price Presentation

The importance of when and how a sales person presents price during the presentation can make a sale or break one. Never give the price until you have established the customer's current situation.

For example, a customer who has an interest in changing to your product may be tied to an agreement that requires an early-termination payment penalty. This payment penalty is often called a "buyout." If you present your price and then find out they have a payment penalty, the customer may focus more on the loss of money for early termination than on the benefits derived from your product. Therefore, your best option is to first establish if there is a payment penalty, and if so, add the amount onto the cost of your product and present the total cost, including the buyout.

The same thought pattern has to be adopted if there's a potential for a trade-in. A customer may want to change to your product but could be uncomfortable making a decision if not receiving anything in return for the current product. Make sure you take advantage of any flexibility in your price so you can use it as a trade-in for the customer's existing product.

Whenever price is mentioned, always replace the word *price* with *investment* because "investment" implies to customers that they will get a return from whatever they are about to buy. The word *investment* is always associated with the positive rather than the negative. Once you have presented the price, always relate back to your customers the matching benefits and the results they will receive by moving forward. This way, after confirming the price, you don't leave them focusing on the cost, which, incidentally, will grow bigger and bigger in their mind.

The positive and confident way in which you present your price will speak volumes to your customer. The following techniques are used extensively by sales pros within their presentation to justify the investment in relation to their customer's situation.

## Price Priming

Price priming mentally prepares your prospective customer for the price you are going to present. It helps to eliminate price shock at the end of your presentation, which can kill the sale. Price priming is a technique usually backed by fear—fear that you have instilled in your customer's mind by educating him about how much it could cost if he waits too long to make the decision. This, of course, will only work if you sound credible and knowledgeable, and is most powerful when used in conjunction with an incentive to buy at that time.

An example of price priming within the automobile industry would be a salesperson's confirming to a prospective customer that he will try to keep the price under a certain figure; for example, $9,000 to buy or $300 per month to lease. Then, after showing the car, he produces a cost of $6,900 or $199 per month. The prospective customer immediately feels as though she is getting a great deal, because she is comparing the price the salesperson has just confirmed with the price previously given.

Price priming also works in reverse. For example, have you ever taken your car in to be considered for a trade-in? First the salesperson asks you how much you want for your car; you confirm a figure of $3,000. Then he walks around the car with you, notes every scratch and dent, shows concern for the high mileage, measures the tread on the tires and finally listens to the engine. Often, by the time he's finished appraising your car, he's made it look so bad that you're grateful for him to offer you anything just to take it off your hands.

The salesperson primes you into thinking that the car is only worth $1,000 and backs it with fear by highlighting all of its problems. If you decide not to trade it for a new car now, you end up worrying that you're going to have to spend a lot of money in the near future on repairs. So if he offers you $2,000 as a trade for your car, you jump at it and drive off in a new vehicle. Remember, the salesperson should be in control at all times.

## Choice of Prices

Presenting a choice of prices is powerful because it gets your prospective customer to focus on a smaller decision than the overall buying decision. Focusing your customer on two or three pricing options ensures that when he decides on one of the choices, he has automatically made the decision to buy. In choice pricing, you could offer a choice of prices for the same product or for different products within your company. Choice pricing also helps to eliminate the likelihood that your prospective customer will get alternative quotes from competitors; you have instead directed his focus toward the two or three pricing options you've presented.

## Reducing the Price Down to the Ridiculous

"Reducing the price down to the ridiculous" means to take the price of your product, work out the finance figure and reduce the figure down to a quarterly, monthly or weekly price. It's easier for the customer to justify buying your product once the price appears lower and more realistic. Five monthly payments of $400 sound better than a one-time payment of $2,000. In addition, once you have worked out your financials, you could relate the figure to your customer in his or her own personal terms. For example, if you know he plays golf, equate the price to golf balls.

If finance isn't an option and your prospective customer is considering the purchase price, then establish how long she anticipates keeping the new product and divide your purchase figure by the length of time she mentions. For example, if the investment is $10,000 and she anticipates keeping the product for four years, divide the $10,000 by four and then by fifty-two. You can then present the price as only $48 per week.

Compare every bouncing bomb to a test question with a positive response. Each bounce gets you nearer and nearer to your goal, until finally, bang! You're there!

## 4) Involving the Senses

Sales pros understand the visual, auditory and kinesthetic sensory elements and know how to involve these senses during their presentation. Although communication occurs using all three of these senses, usually one will stand out and become a more important factor in how each specific person comprehends information. Involving all the senses is a communication technique that speeds up the ability to connect your customer to what you are trying to communicate. Listening to what your customer is saying will offer you the knowledge of what direction to take in your presentation; and although vision is important, your ability to identify a strong auditory or kinesthetic tendency will allow you to connect with your customer faster and more effectively.

1. *Visual:* A picture paints a thousand words, so whenever you can, use visuals to explain what you are saying to offer quicker comprehension for customers who have a stronger tendency to learn through seeing. The golden rule of visual information is to always look at what you are showing and not at your customer; that way, your customer will be inclined to look at the solution you're presenting instead of watching you.

2. *Auditory:* If your product has low noise volume, focusing your customer on how quietly it operates will offer quicker comprehension of the information for customers who have a stronger tendency to learn through hearing.

3. *Kinesthetic:* Handing your product or details of your product to your prospective customer, getting them to push the start button or actively involving them in the presentation will offer quicker comprehension of information for customers who have a stronger tendency to learn through feeling and touching.

# Examples of Reducing the Price Down to the Ridiculous

## Purchase Example

| Purchase Example | Your Product Purchase Price | Expected Product Life Expectancy or Term | Annual Investment | Weekly Investment |
|---|---|---|---|---|
| First Company | $10,000 | 4 Years | $10,000 Divided By 4 = $2,500 Per Year | $2,500 Divided By 52 = $48 Per Week |

## Finance Example

| Finance Example | Your Product Annual Finance Price | Monthly Finance Investment | Weekly | Daily Investment |
|---|---|---|---|---|
| Investment | $3,000 Per Year | $3,000 Divided By 12 = $250 Per Month | $250 Divided By 4 = $62.50 Per Week | $62.50 Divided By 5 Business Days = $12.50 Per Day |

## Difference Pricing

Difference pricing is where you establish the difference between the price of your product and the price of the product your prospective customer is already using or what he may also be considering. You focus only on the difference. For example, if your price is $100 per month, and he is currently paying $80 per month, talk only of the $20 monthly difference.

You could say, "Mr. Jones, we are talking about a difference of only $20 per month for what is recognized as being the best product available for you. This equates to only five dollars per week. Surely for the added benefits [this is where you explain the additional matching benefits he will obtain by changing to your product], and knowing you will be using this product for at least the next three years, one dollar a day is not too much to pay."

## Competitor's Pricing Disadvantage

| Purchase Example | Your Product Purchase Price | Competitors Purchase Price | Purchase Difference | Anticipated Product Life Expectancy or Term | Difference Breakdown to Annual, Monthly & Weekly | Your Justification |
|---|---|---|---|---|---|---|
| Investment | $20,000 | $17,000 | $3,000 | 4 Years | $3,000 Divided By 48 Months= $62.50 Per Month, $15.62 Per Week | Your Added Benefits and/or Differentiation |

## Finance Example

| Finance Example | Your Annual Product Finance Price | Competitor's Annual Finance Price | Annual Finance Difference | Monthly Difference | Weekly Difference | Your Justification |
|---|---|---|---|---|---|---|
| Investment | $12,500 Per Year | $9,600 Per Year | $2,900 Per Year | $2,900 Divided By 12 = $241.66 Per Month | $241.66 Divided By 4 = $60.41 Per Week Additional Investment | Your Added Benefits and/or Differentiation |

This can also work in reverse. If your price is less than your competitor's, expand the price difference: Multiply the difference by the amount of time he anticipates keeping the new product, and discuss what additional benefits he will be getting in addition to the amount he will be saving. For example, if your price is $100 per week and your competitor's is $125 per week, and the potential customer anticipates keeping the new product for three years, take the $25 difference and multiply it by fifty-two and then by three. You could say, "Mr. Jones, over the three years you anticipate keeping this product, you will save $3,900 and have the advantage of all the additional benefits." You would then list the additional matching benefits and results he will receive by committing to your product.

## Finance Pricing Advantage

| Finance Example | Your Annual Product Finance Price | Competitor's Annual Finance Price | Your Annual Finance Difference Advantage | Anticipated Product Life Expectancy or Term | Total Pricing Advantage |
|---|---|---|---|---|---|
| Investment | $12,000 Per Year | $15,000 Per Year | $3,000 Per Year | 5 Years | $3,000 Times 5 Years = $15,000 Savings |

## Price Objection Examples

Four proposed responses to "I can buy it for less elsewhere" are outlined below.

"I Can Buy It For Less Elsewhere."

1. "Yes, Mr. Jones, but is price your most important consideration? Most people consider value equally important; wouldn't you agree? Let me explain why our product offers you the best value."

2. "Mr. Jones, when you need an attorney or a doctor, do you base your decision regarding your choice solely on how much she charges? You'd be concerned with reputation, level of expertise and service, wouldn't you?"

3. "Yes, Mr. Jones, but how much less? How long do you expect it to last? For only X dollars more a day, you could afford to have the best."

4. "Mr. Jones, you have asked for a product that will enable you to be 30 percent more productive, which is why the investment is an additional $45 per week. If it were any less, we wouldn't be able to offer you exactly what you are looking for. You do want to increase your productivity and still maintain the quality, don't you?"

## 7) Reason to Buy Today

The sales pro always offers a "reason to buy today." The "reason to buy today," however, should only be the icing on the cake. It is never the main reason for confirming the order. The reasons to buy at the time of your presentation should help support the decision to commit to something the customer was going to commit to anyway, but it potentially increases her sense of urgency to say yes and shortens the sale's time frame. Information on incentives, discounts or delivery schedules could be used as reasons for your customer to move forward today; never volunteer this information too early. Although you may have offered an excellent return on investment and left no reason for your customer to say no, most people need that underlying reason or incentive to say yes. It's human nature to want to get not just getting the right product, but a great deal, too.

You must be creative and believable when presenting a reason to move forward today. This means tapping into emotional selling and thinking about various angles that allow you to control when your prospective customer will buy. Offering a discount is the easiest form of trying to control the timing of the sale, but because it's so overused, this does not lend you much credibility. Therefore, look at your product and take time to work out what additional items you could offer in place of a discount, such as the threat of a future price increase or low stock, which would affect them if they didn't move forward today, quick delivery, which would ensure they immediately realize the benefits of the new product, or additional free features that you can offer if they decide to move forward within a specific time frame. Always remember to prequalify the sale before giving anything away. Prequalification means to make sure that the customer is aware she must move forward with the order to achieve the benefits described. If you don't prequalify, you could find yourself providing the additional item or trade-in and receiving the dreaded words, "I'll think about it."

# PRICE
# PRESENTATION

## CARTOON STORY

BUT WOULDN'T THE CUSTOMER ASK FOR THE FINANCE FIGURE IF YOU JUST QUOTED THE PRICE?

THAT'S JUST IT. REMEMBER, YOU HAVE CONTROL. IT'S ALL ABOUT HOW YOU PRESENT THE PRICE.
IF YOU LEAD WITH THE PURCHASE PRICE, THAT'S WHAT STAYS IN THEIR MIND. IF YOU LEAD WITH THE FINANCE FIGURE, THEN THAT'S WHAT STAYS IN THEIR MIND.

THAT SOUNDS GREAT! I'M GOING TO WORK OUT THE FINANCE FIGURE OF ALL MY PRODUCTS SO I CAN LEAD WITH FINANCE - IT'S SURE TO INCREASE MY SALES!

AHH! SO THAT MENTALLY IT GETS THEM THINKING OF JUST THE ADDITIONAL AMOUNT THEY WOULD HAVE TO INVEST, INSTEAD OF REMINDING THEM OF THE WHOLE OVERALL PRICE!

ABSOLUTELY! AND REMEMBER...

YOU'VE GOT IT! AND YOU MENTIONED THE WORD "INVEST". . . THAT'S EXCELLENT. ALWAYS REFER TO YOUR PRICE AS AN INVESTMENT. IT MENTALLY TELLS THE CUSTOMER THAT THEY WILL BE BENEFITTING IN THE FUTURE.

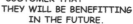

... LEARN YOUR WEEKLY COSTS FROM MEMORY, IT'S SO MUCH MORE POWERFUL. ALSO, WHEN YOU'RE PRICING AGAINST THEIR EXISTING SYSTEM, ALWAYS TALK OF JUST THE DIFFERENCE BETWEEN YOUR COST AND THEIRS.

OH YES, ONE OTHER POINT. . . AFTER QUOTING THE PRICE, ALWAYS RECAP THE MATCHING BENEFITS AND THEN ASSUME THE SALE.

WHY IS THAT?

BECAUSE THEN YOU DON'T LEAVE YOUR CUSTOMER JUST THINKING OF THE PRICE. INSTEAD THEY HAVE TO THINK OF WHAT THEY WILL BE GETTING.

AND THEN ASSUME THE SALE?

YES, AND IF THEY QUESTION IT, YOU SHOULD RECAP HOW THEY WILL BENEFIT BY GOING AHEAD, AND ADD A REASON TO BUY TODAY.

GREAT! I'M OFF TO PRACTICE WITH JOHN RIGHT AFTER I'VE WORKED MY FINANCE FIGURES OUT.

## Profile of a Presentation

The following nine diagrams offer a visual review of how a presentation takes shape as a sales pro incorporates the seven specific sales techniques that create the presentation structure. A sales pro covers the full presentation platform and strategically outlines when and where she'll incorporate the techniques. Based on the information she has gathered, she then presents a customized, interactive experience, which she knows will be of interest to her customer.

Each diagram explains the timing of when a specific sales technique should be introduced, offering a visual reinforcement of the progression of the presentation from the very start to finally seeking customer commitment and closing the sale.

### Diagram One

Diagram one shows the initial stages of the presentation. The sales pro is presenting one of her products, which has six potential benefits. In order to identify which benefits her customer will be interested in, she has asked twelve questions. She has also completed her presentation platform, which consisted of decision-maker confirmation, a reintroduction of her company and product, a recap of the information she gathered previously and the presentation of the general benefit statement.

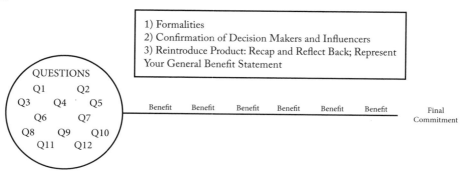

## Diagram Two

Diagram two shows the advancement of the presentation. After asking the initial twelve questions, the sales pro has identified three matching benefits; these will be the focus for the presentation and ensure it is customized to her customer. The matching benefits are still in the sales pro's mind, and each one will be presented to the customer strategically during the presentation.

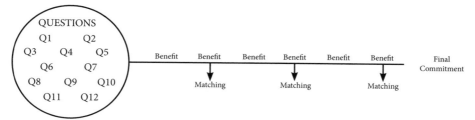

## Diagram Three

Diagram three shows the timing of when the sales pro has decided to present her first matching benefit, which was identified from the answers received when she asked her customer questions four and eight.

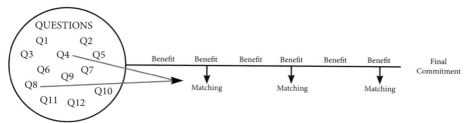

## Diagram Four

Diagram four shows the timing of when the sales pro decides to present the second matching benefit that was identified from the answer she received to question number seven.

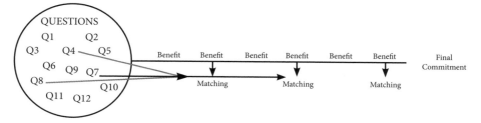

## Diagram Five

Diagram five shows the timing of when the sales pro is asking her first test-close question. Two of the matching benefits have been presented; the sales pro is now testing the waters to confirm the customer's commitment level.

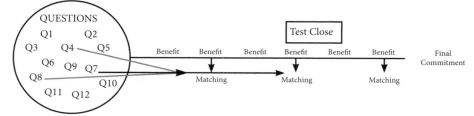

## Diagram Six

Diagram six shows the timing of when the sales pro is presenting her third matching benefit. The need for the solution this benefit matches was identified from the answers the sales pro received to questions one and five. The sales pro has also chosen to appeal to the customer's kinesthetic sense by getting her customer physically involved in the presentation.

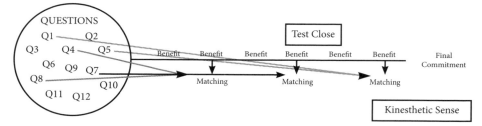

## Diagram Seven

Diagram seven identifies when the sales pro has chosen to incorporate her customer's emotional reason for buying. She has also decided to test her customer's commitment level through a second test close.

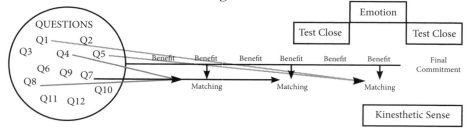

## Diagram Eight

Diagram eight shows the timing of when the sales pro has chosen to introduce her price.

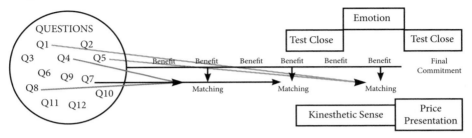

## Diagram Nine

Diagram nine shows the completed profile of the presentation. The sales pro asked twelve questions; out of the six potential benefits her product offers, she identified and presented three that match her customer's needs and raised the perception of each matching benefit before presenting it. She test-closed twice, involved a kinesthetic sense and emotional connection, presented the price and offered a reason to make an immediate buying decision. Now the sales pro can move forward and assume or ask for final customer commitment.

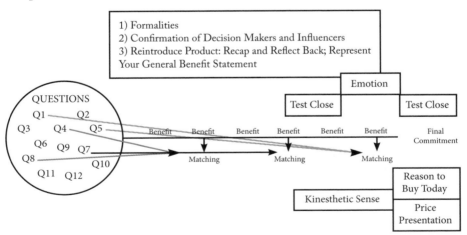

## Satisfied Customers

A satisfied customer is your number one asset, and your ability to establish a positive relationship after you have made a sale is another trait to master. The ultimate presentation should yield a satisfied customer who then presents the product to another of your prospective customers.

Therefore, as you retain new customers, use them to your advantage. Once you have a customer who has been using your product for a period of time and has been able to achieve the results you promised, ask him if you can bring a prospective customer to his office in order to show how the product works within his operation. After all, anyone who makes a good decision wants to talk about it. If he is agreeable, count yourself that much closer to the sale. Let your customer do the talking and take a step back, allowing your prospective customer and current customer to discuss details between themselves.

## Self-Assessment

List five of your most satisfied customers. List why they are satisfied.

**Customer**                    **Reason for Satisfaction**

1) _____      _____

2) _____      _____

3) _____      _____

4) _____      _____

5) _____      _____

# EIGHT

# The Power of Objections

## Using Objections to Progress the Sale

You will encounter objections during every stage of the sales process. Sales pros understand what's behind the objections, learn how to overcome them and whenever possible use them to move the sale forward. They also know that poor selling creates objections; for example, you can have two people selling the same product and yet one will get twice as many objections as the other. The main reasons an objection will occur are due to inadequate gathering of information before a meeting, a poor presentation or presenting to someone who is not the decision maker. This last objection is the most common, especially among sales people who are so excited to present their product that they often forget to confirm if the person they are presenting to can make a decision.

So how do you reduce the possibility of using all your energy to complete an enthusiastic and well-performed presentation to someone who cannot make a decision? Through prequalification! A sales pro always makes it her job to know her audience and will ask the person or people she is about to present to what part of the buying process they are responsible for.

Always ensure that your presentation is being given to someone who will be able to make a decision at the end of it—not necessarily the decision to buy, but the decision to move forward with the *possibility* of buying. The day you make this a commitment is the day you will become more effective in overcoming objections and mastering the art of selling.

Objections come up frequently and should not surprise you; it's your job to dig deeper to gain further understanding of the reason for the objection or, more importantly, to ascertain if it's an objection or a condition.

So, what exactly is an objection and what is a condition? Both are reasons why someone isn't moving forward to the next stage of the sale. Sometimes objections are real, and sometimes they aren't. Sometimes there is one and other times there are many. An objection is a problem you can overcome, whereas you can't overcome a condition. Say you are presenting a product that has a specific motor size and your prospective customer says the size of the motor does not offer the speed they require. If you have other motor options that will increase the speed, then you know that the objection can be overcome. If, however, you cannot offer a different motor, then speed now becomes a condition.

During the sales process, you will find that objections are much more common than conditions. When you find yourself in this position, your challenge will be to ask open questions to help identify the difference so you know how to respond. However, there will also be times when the condition can be minimized to a difficult objection; the strategy then becomes to focus on what benefits outweigh the difficult objection and positioning a different thought process with your customer. Below are examples of objections and conditions to make you more aware of the difference between the two.

| Objections | Conditions |
| --- | --- |
| "I want to look at the competition." | "I have no money." |
| "I don't like the color." | "I don't have space." |
| "I want to think it over." | "I can't get financing." |

A sales person will be tested every day with new objections or problems. The idea is to remember previous objections or questions that you couldn't answer, so that when you find out from your manager or colleague what you could or should have said, you will be able to respond accordingly in the future. This is why it's important to know about all of your products, their additional options and anything else that is relevant, like backup service, support or product flexibility.

For example, if you don't know that you can reduce the size or change the color of your product, how are you going to overcome these objections when they're posed by prospective customers? You'll end up treating their objections as conditions (i.e., problems you can't change), which in turn will mean that you'll miss out on opportunities to move the sale forward.

It is critical that you have knowledge about your competitors. If you do not, and your prospective customer says he wants to look at a different company's product before making a decision, he has a legitimate objection. For you, the fact that he also wants to see your competitors is a condition. You can go over the selling points of your product and company again, and then try to get commitment for the sale. But you're often swimming against the tide.

Make it your job to know about all the other products your competition offers so that when confronted with an objection, you can handle it deftly. Specifically, you should ask which particular model the prospective customer is going to consider. Get out the competitor's brochure and your fact sheet to compare, point out how the competitor's model is less superior, focus on your differentiation, explain why the only consideration should be your product, and advance the sale.

Below is an example for you to follow.

SALES PRO: "Mr. Jones, I understand why you want to consider [your competitor's product]. You are making an important decision. Tell me, is this the only other product you are considering?"

CUSTOMER: "Yes." [If at this point he says no, clarify which other products he is also considering.]

| SALES PRO: | "Well, Mr. Jones, the way I understand it, if you had already seen the other product, you would be able to make your decision now, wouldn't you?" |
|---|---|
| CUSTOMER: | "Yes." [If at this point he says no, ask what else would be stopping him.] |
| SALES PRO: | "Mr. Jones, is there anything else that you would need our product to do?" |
| CUSTOMER: | "No." |
| SALES PRO: | "Is there anything that my product offers that you don't feel you need?" |
| CUSTOMER: | "No." |
| SALES PRO: | "Mr. Jones, I make it my job to know as much as possible about our industry. This in turn helps me to help my customers. Let me show you the facts about the product you are also considering." |

Have as much information regarding your competitors' products as possible, and be knowledgeable regarding the differences between your company and products and those of your competition. You should effectively re-explain to your customer how your product and company differentiation separates you from your competition, and reconfirm the value of the differentiation in terms of the return on investment he would obtain, in addition to the other results he would realize by buying your product.

## The Power of *Feel, Felt* and *Found*

There are many techniques open to a salesperson regarding how to initially respond to an objection or condition. One very effective technique is the power of *feel, felt* and *found,* which enables a salesperson to gain more time in order to absorb the objection before answering it.

This technique involves using the words *feel, felt* and *found* in a sentence followed by an assumed or alternative commitment. Assuming commitment means assuming that your prospective customer will move forward with the sale or to the next stage of the cycle. The alternative commitment involves asking questions with specific alternatives that lead to a sale.

THE POWER OF OBJECTIONS | 147

Check out the example below of a salesperson asking for an appointment:

CUSTOMER:     "I don't need one."

SALES PRO:     "I appreciate how you **feel**, Mr. Jones. In fact, many similar companies to yours **felt** exactly the same way before they heard what I had to say. What they **found** after meeting with me, however, was that my product was useful and the potential results they would be able to achieve were a sufficient reason to consider it. The initial appointment takes only twenty minutes, and I will already be in the area next week talking to a few other companies."

## Easy Objections and Difficult Objections

Easy objections occur when you can meet the customer's need. If you can't meet the need and the customer confirms the given feature is important, then it becomes a difficult objection and potentionally a condition. It will, however, depend on how the customer responds when asked how important a particular feature is; sometimes what the salesperson thinks is potentially a difficult objection is not. Instead, it's just a question.

It is imperative that whenever you encounter any objection, you absorb it like a sponge and never look concerned or inflate its importance. The more worried you look and the more you react to an objection, the more your prospective customer will try to establish why you are concerned—even if he didn't feel this objection was that important in the first place. This could cost you the opportunity for a sale. Remain calm and understanding when handling objections. Put yourself in the customer's shoes and look at the objection as though it were your own. Confirm to him that you understand and care about what he has said. And regardless of whether it's an easy or difficult objection, always be sympathetic with what he has objected to.

What a sales person will often see as a major disadvantage or objection, a sales pro will turn into a customer's reason for buying. Look closely at the situation at hand, and you can create some interesting reasons why what the customer thought was a disadvantage is, in fact, a good reason she should buy.

The keys are assuming that her concern is important and using the techniques outlined in the following paragraphs to overcome potential objections.

Following are two techniques, one for handling easy objections and one for difficult objections. The steps outlined within each technique will help you identify whether the objection is legitimate. It could simply be camouflage for not wanting to commit straightaway or a sign that your customer needs more information.

The technique for responding to an easy objection takes advantage of the fact that you can do what your customer is asking; however, instead of just responding "Yes, we can," rephrase it so that you achieve a commitment to move forward.

### Easy Objections

1. Rephrase the objection, and acknowledge your understanding and agreement of the concern.

2. Confirm that if you can do what he is asking, he will move forward.

For example:

| | |
|---|---|
| CUSTOMER: | "Does it come in blue?" |
| SALES PRO: | "That's an interesting question, Mr. Jones. Why would you want it in blue?" |
| CUSTOMER: | "The company color is blue." |
| SALES PRO: | "So the reason you need it in blue is because your company color is blue and it's important that the product matches. Is that correct?" |
| CUSTOMER: | "Yes." |
| SALES PRO: | "Mr. Jones, if I can supply it in blue, would you like to move forward?" |
| CUSTOMER: | "Yes." |

The technique for handling a difficult objection is obviously more detailed and involves minimizing the objection, isolating it and maximizing the reasons why it would be advantageous to move forward. This technique is not designed to push your customer into a corner or make him feel intimidated or awkward. Rather, its purpose is to redirect your customer's thought process so that he reconsiders all the advantages he will be receiving, which could outweigh his concern over the one specific aspect he feels he needs.

**Difficult Objections**

1. Rephrase the objection, and acknowledge your understanding and agreement of the concern.

2. Isolate the objection.

3. Ask for clarification of why the objection is so important.

4. Tell a third-party story of a previous customer who benefitted by moving forward despite originally needing an additional feature your product did not offer.

5. Minimize the objection, maximize the matching benefits and reconfirm the results and financial gain you agreed he would obtain.

"Third party" is a term used for another person or company who is not associated with the people who are in discussion. For example, the salesperson may share a story with their customer about how another customer benefitted from their product after committing. The salesperson may have another story of a previous customer who was also hesitant because the product didn't exactly match her needs; however, the other advantages she received from using the product far outweighed the fact that the product did not achieve the other needs she was after.

Let's say matching the customer's color was a difficult objection, in that you didn't have the product available in blue. The example below gives you an idea of what would follow after you had rephrased the objection and acknowledged your understanding and agreement of the customer's concern.

SALES PRO: "Apart from the fact that it isn't blue, is there anything else stopping you from moving forward?"

CUSTOMER: "I don't think so."

SALES PRO: "Just to clarify, Mr. Jones, why is matching the company color so important?"

It is at this point that your prospective customer could say to you, "Well, it isn't *extremely* important that it matches, although it would be nice. I was just interested to know." Such a response would mean you can reduce the importance of the objection by simply explaining you don't have it in blue, offer an alternative choice of color, reinforce the results he will receive and assume the sale or progression to the next stage of the sale.

If, however, he tells you why the color is very important, you could respond in the following way:

CUSTOMER: "Well, it's always an important consideration."

SALES PRO: "I agree. In fact, I've helped out many companies with this particular product, and one of them had purchased their previous product because of the importance of color. They actually missed out on a couple of advantages because they felt the color was that important. When I showed them how much it was costing them and how much they could save if color was not an issue, however, the savings and advantages simply outweighed the need to match the brand. The irony was that the company rebranded a year later and changed its color anyway."

CUSTOMER: "Really? that's interesting."

SALES PRO: "Although we are not able to exactly match the color, why don't we focus on the new advantages your company will receive and the immediate cost savings you'd achieve by moving forward. I can meet your ideal delivery time, and I know you are aware of the tremendous company benefits and immediate return on investment."

The psychology behind this example is that you are creating a story—true or not—that resonates with the prospective customer. The story's point then makes it extremely difficult for the prospective customer to justify proceeding with his objection and will make him re-question his original thought.

Remember to use your personality, charm and charisma. You can see how important these qualities become not only in closing the sale but in overcoming difficult objections, which thwart progression of the sale. Although you are using commonsense phrases to win over your prospective customer, the emotional element can never be underestimated. Remember, people buy people first and whatever else second. This is true no matter what you're selling.

## Practice

Prospective customers will undoubtedly test your patience with objections. Objections are a fact of life and you'll get them every day. Prepare yourself by establishing which objections you get regularly; write them down and then work out your best responses so that you have answers ready. Having a response that will get you closer to the sale will give you confidence every time you're faced with an objection. Then rehearse the responses so you sound authentic and natural.

Always practice your responses with a second person. Once you answer her objection, let your partner give her natural response. Stop and think about an answer to that response, write it down and respond back again. You should feel comfortable with your responses. After all, your end goal is to walk away with the sale or advance the sale, so you have to make your responses flow naturally into confirmation that he will move forward or buy. You may well get objections that need two or three answers, which will allow you to approach the objection at an angle that is right for your prospective customer.

## Exercise

Write down two of the most common objections you hear from customers and two possible responses to each of them.

OBJECTION 1

First response: _____

Second response: _____


OBJECTION 2

First response: _____

Second response: _____

# HANDLING OBJECTIONS

## CARTOON STORY

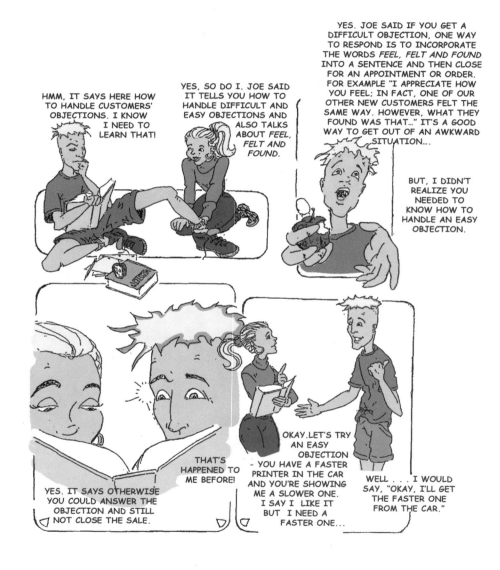

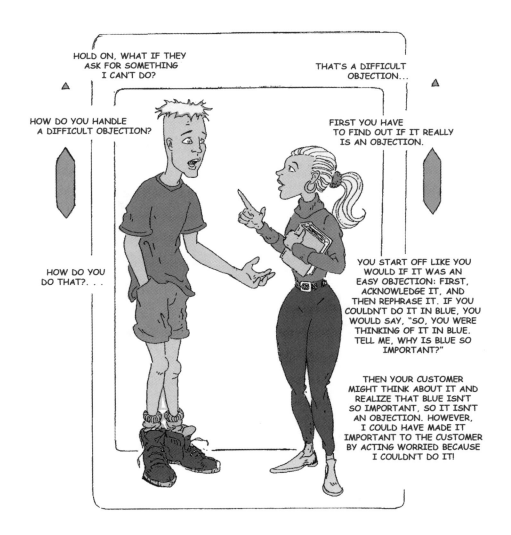

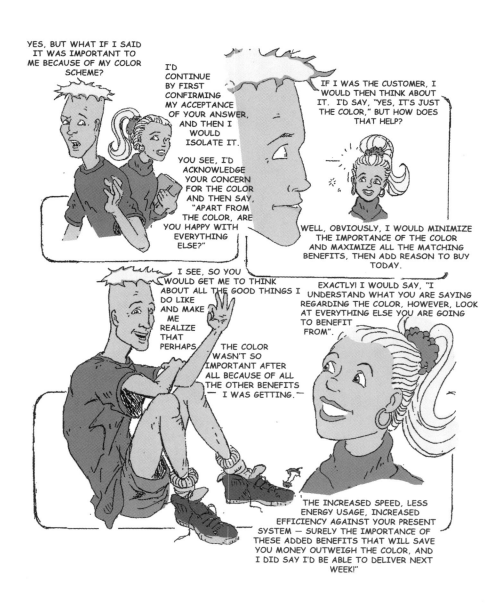

# NINE

## Closing the Sale

### Final Customer Commitment

The last stage of the sales cycle is called closing the sale or achieving final commitment, which means the customer has confirmed she will buy.

Many people who enter into the world of sales go searching for a magic ingredient that will help them achieve more sales. The problem is that a magic ingredient doesn't exist. It's rarely ever one quick or clever sentence that enables your prospective customer to say yes. Sales pros know you must first open the mind of your prospective customer, gain their trust and emotionally achieve their acceptance ("buy-in") to commit to the sale.

### Trust

Complete customer commitment is an accumulation of every interaction you have had with your customer, from your very first telephone call or meeting to the time when you are ready to ask for their signature to move forward. The fundamental trigger in the mind of your prospective customer will be trust: trust in what you are saying and in the result you are saying they will receive.

Take an example of a salesperson selling dollar bills (crazy as it sounds). The salesperson offers you $20 for your $5 bill or $50 for your $20. Who would say no? But what if the salesperson was offering you $100 for your $100? Or $750 for your $500? Your decision is going to change in relation to the perceived value of what is being presented. Why? The psychology behind the thought process changes with each decision.

The $5 and $20 decisions were low risk to the customer, so you'd expect little thought and quick decision. But in the $100 for $100 situation, the salesperson offered something that yields no value to the customer, so why should the customer accept? The fourth option of giving $500 to receive $750 provides great value, but requires more investment—in time, money and trust—from the customer. Due to the size of the transaction and what could be the potential loss of $500, the customer needs more time to think about the decision, and also needs to have more trust in the seller. Reasonably, the prospective customer now has questions before committing: Are the dollar bills real? Who is this salesperson and why is he offering this to me?

The deal might sound solid to the prospective customer, but now the salesperson needs a story to get the customer to commit. The story has to be authentic, confirm there is little to no risk, and reconfirm the customer will absolutely receive the result promised. The story needed for one-call customer commitments are very different than for sales that require multiple calls before customer commitment is achieved. This is due to the level of trust that needs to develop and the amount of information that needs to be exchanged.

How do you achieve the necessary trust? It should be gained throughout your entire interaction with your prospective customer, reinforced first and foremost by the belief you show in how your product will absolutely benefit your potential customer in a way that no other company or product can. Trust is also achieved by building rapport; using sensory system dialogue that links with your prospective customer's kinesthetic, auditory or visual communication styles; using sources like testimonial letters or outside statistics that confirm what you have said; and thoroughly educating your potential customer.

Sales pros always focus on educating their customers, whereas average performers focus their potential customers on fear of losing out or on a marketing program that is due to expire. Both tactics can be effective in the short term but never in the long term. Your ability to educate your customer on why you believe your solution is the best option and how it will give them the results you have presented is the underlying objective that creates the connection to make them want what you are offering. The more you show how educated you are, not just about your product and their situation but about your industry, the more confident they will feel in moving forward. Show your commitment to the field you are in by sharing market trends, research and future vision against past history, highlighting how significant the differences are or will be. Doing so reinforces your knowledge, enthusiasm and passion, which creates trust and enables your customer to feel comfortable not just making a decision but the right decision that she believes will give her the best results.

Powerful questioning techniques that push customers into a corner and make them feel stupid if they do not move forward are outdated and not recommended. Your job is to help a decision move forward that you believe is the absolute best option for your potential customers. If you are a true professional and believe in what you are selling, the techniques presented within this chapter will increase your confidence in completing the sale.

## Preparation from the Start

Closing a sale by asking for final customer commitment can be awkward if, during the early sale stages, the prospective customer considered you more of a consultant, a friend or a helper than a salesperson. This can happen because in the early stages of any sale, you rarely ask your prospective customer for anything that could lead to conflict (e.g., money or a signed commitment). What you are doing instead is absolutely everything you can to win her over to your product and your way of thinking.

Now you're at the stage where you are asking the customer to agree to hand over the money or sign the agreement. Keep in mind that at this stage your prospective customer should not feel any hesitation to buy or feel intimidated into signing the agreement or handing over the money, since you have established that they can trust that what you have presented will offer what the customer is after. However, it goes without saying that money matters to everyone, and even the most committed people can change their minds and behavior when money is involved. Whether company money or your own, everyone knows the importance of it. Therefore, it's imperative that you mentally, physically and emotionally prepare your prospective customer for the commitment from the start of the first call to when you ask for her commitment to move forward. During every step of the way, consistently reconfirm how your product will benefit the company or individual. This reinforcement keeps all the decision makers and influencers focused on the result they will achieve with your product, as well as the knowledge that their investment will be counteracted by the value and return on investment they will be receiving. The majority of the sale is always made before the presentation is ever given, which reinforces the need to ensure that every stage of the sales process has been covered thoroughly before you attempt to ask for or assume the order. Make sure you have identified all the influencers and decision makers and have taken the opportunity to educate them on the potential value and return on investment they and their company will receive with your product. It's critical to incorporate their feedback from your questions into your presentation so they feel included in what you are asking them to commit to.

## Fear

Asking for final commitment should be the easiest and most natural question you will ask of your potential customer, and yet due to fear of rejection, it's often the hardest.

Fear of rejection is the most common reason a sales person will not ask for the order. After all, you've had no rejection up to this point in the sales process, and you've been doing everything you can to impress them; now you might get a "no." "No" is as bad as it gets, but it should never be taken personally. Your prospective customer is potentially saying no to your product, not to you as a person.

It's your responsibility to eliminate all the potential obstacles so you don't receive a negative response. But inevitably this situation will occur. The idea is to have it happen less often than more often. Keep in mind that people respect others who are professional enough to ask for something, especially if they have complete belief in what they are proposing and feel equally as sure that their prospective customer will benefit.

## Closing Commitment Techniques

The following techniques are geared more toward short sales cycles; however, a gentle tweak allows them to be incorporated at the appropriate time into specific stages or the final stage of the longer sale cycle. Note that some of these techniques are to be used only if the salesperson can offer what the customer is asking for.

Most people need to be asked for the commitment and are uncomfortable if they are left requesting the documentation or your pen in order to complete the paperwork. Be sincere and authentic and create the mindset that you are only asking for their business because you genuinely believe they will benefit.

**Closing Technique**

## Assuming the Sale Technique

The most powerful commitment technique you can use throughout your presentation is to assume the sale or assume the next stage of the sale. The technique's transition (from no commitment to commitment) is natural, smooth and subtle. The psychological tendency for a person watching someone else assume something is to naturally go with it, especially if the logic makes sense. If there is no reason to not move forward, the customer feels relieved to let the decision be taken out of his hands. There is comfort in knowing that the person helping make the decision for you is absolutely sure in what it will offer; they are moving forward without hesitation, which prompts you to do so, as well.

Assumption also eliminates the need to ask a question, which could trigger your prospective customer to think more than they need to, creating a needless barrier. Therefore, don't get to the end of your presentation and create an immediate barrier by asking for commitment to move forward; just assume it!

Gear your interaction and conversations with your prospective customer as though they already own your product and are benefitting from it. This creates a platform so that after all the hard work of finding your prospective customer, gathering information, preparing the right product, establishing matching benefits, arranging the time for the presentation and making sure all the decision makers are there, you flow naturally into the assumption of moving forward.

For example: "Mr. Jones, I'm going to arrange for all the paperwork to be automatically e-mailed to you. I just need a high-resolution image of your company logo for the advertising and the 10 percent deposit check."

The average sales performer does not usually assume the order or even ask for it because of fear of rejection. They wait for the customer to say, "I'll take it." Unfortunately this rarely happens. Take control and assume your prospective customer is going to move forward. Doing so reinforces your belief that they are going to benefit exactly as you have presented and will trigger your customer to move forward without thought or doubt.

## Alternative Commitment Technique

The alternative commitment technique involves asking questions with specific alternatives that lead to a sale. Take this question: "Would you like your coffee with one sugar or two?" Most people would answer either "One" or "Two," or "I don't take sugar in coffee." They may not have even wanted a drink, or preferred tea to the coffee, but because of the question's phrasing, the customer is more likely to accept the coffee as offered. The idea is to direct the customer's focus away from the major decision of the coffee (what you want them to buy) and towards the smaller decision of the sugar (a different result that flows from having bought the product).

For example: "Ms. Smith, would you like delivery this week or would next week be better for you?" This sentence focuses Ms. Smith on thinking about what week to accept delivery; her answer will confirm to the salesperson she has committed to buy. The salesperson can now move forward by asking for her bank details or credit card to get the paperwork completed so the agreed-upon delivery can be documented.

## Easy Question Technique

Use the easy question technique when you get a question from your prospective customer to which you know you can answer "yes." Instead of volunteering the answer, use this technique to gain further commitment or achieve the sale. Three examples are given below:

| Prospective Customer | Salespro |
| --- | --- |
| "Can you deliver in three days?" | "Can we move forward if I can?" |
| "Does it come in blue?" | "If I can get it in blue, will you order?" |
| "Do you offer financing?" | "If I can provide financing, can we move forward?" |

The assumed, alternative, and easy-question commitment techniques have all been designed so that a positive answer to your question confirms the sale or progression to the next stage of the sale. The techniques are only effective if you can do what your prospective customer is asking for, and a salesperson would only use the techniques if he could offer what the customer wants.

During the sales cycle, the timing of when you use these techniques is critical. Take the following example: Your prospective customer asks, "Can it go any faster?" If you get asked a question like this at the beginning of a presentation, it would be wise not to use it as an opportunity to ask for their commitment because it is too early in the sales process and would cause undue pressure on the prospective customer. Instead of answering "Yes, it does; all you do is turn this switch," ask them why they are inquiring, and then tell them that you will cover that point later in the presentation.

When you feel the time is right in the presentation, you can reintroduce the point by saying, "Mr. Jones, earlier you asked if this system could go faster. Could you remind me the reason that speed is important to you?" Listen to their explanation and add another question if necessary to build the importance of what they have said. Then continue, "Mr. Jones, if I can show you that the speed can be increased, would you like to move forward?" If the answer is yes, then show the increased speed and assume the sale. If the answer is no, then show the increase in speed and continue on with the matching benefits and wait for another opportunity to ask for the order.

## Similar Situation Technique

The similar situation technique is used if you have already asked for commitment and your prospective customer is hesitant. The technique becomes a small presentation designed to bring your prospective customer around to your way of thinking without conveying an intimidating attitude.

In the similar situation technique, you tell your prospective customer what happened to a previous potential customer who decided to wait, who decided not to move forward, or who was undecided but then did move forward. Always use real-life situations that you can relate to your prospective customer;

the reality of your belief will make your request for their commitment that much more powerful.

An example of a more detailed request for a customer commitment is the one frequently requested by the classic insurance salesperson. They have been taught to say the following to a hesitant buyer:

"I appreciate that you are unsure at this time; after all, it's an important decision, and I would be hesitant too. However, the only reason I persist is because I want you to be insured from this very moment. I was at a house just a few weeks ago, in a similar situation with someone who was also undecided. Unfortunately, I couldn't convince him to take the disability insurance policy on straightaway, which would have allowed him to be insured that evening, giving his family security from that very moment. I found out yesterday that he was in an accident and will be off work for four months."

Now the customer hearing this story can imagine what financial situation the man's family has been left in, and relates to the feeling of not wanting his family to undergo the same situation. He's more likely to accept the sale because of this. This example helps to illustrate the power of a story, whether it's a negative or positive one.

## "I'll Think About It" Technique

 "I'll think about it" is probably the most common objection you will have to overcome, and it occurs as a result of your customer being hesitant or not buying into the value of what you have presented.

People will typically say, "I want to think about it" if they are either:

1) confused,     2) doubtful    or     3) insecure.

They use this cover-up phrase instead of telling you the real reason, either because they are too embarrassed or don't want to say no. It is at this stage that a confrontation could occur between the salesperson and the prospective customer, because the prospective customer is potentially saying, "I'm not sure I trust what you are saying." This is the last thing the salesperson wants to hear.

Design a response that authentically and sincerely communicates your absolute belief that your prospective customer will benefit by moving forward. Your response will be different every time in terms of intonation, animation and commitment, but the content that creates the platform for your response should be similar. Keep in mind that the smaller the sale, the more impactful your platform response will be.

Following are three examples of a response you could use when a prospective customer says, "I'll think about it." These phrases will help define the true reason why a prospective customer is avoiding the final commitment and will trigger a response from him that gives you something tangible to work with.

### Example 1

"I appreciate that you want to think about it, Mr. Jones. It's an important decision and you wouldn't be thinking about it unless you were really interested, would you? Can I ask what it is that you feel you need more time to think about? [Pause for a reply and then continue straight into the next sentence.] Is it the size? [Pause for a reply.] Is it the color? [Pause for a reply.] Is the speed fast enough for you? [Pause for a reply.] Are you happy with our company? [Pause for a reply.] Do you feel comfortable with me? [Pause for a reply.]"

Always give him enough time to answer each question. Don't give him the opportunity to say, "I just want to think about everything." Go over each individual matching benefit again, and get his confirmation that he is happy with all the benefits. This confirmation will create doubt in his mind as to why, if he is happy and in agreement with everything you have said, he still needs to think about committing.

### Example 2

"Mr. Jones, in my experience, usually when someone is happy with my product, my company and me yet still wants to think about it, it's because he is unsure of one or two points. Is that how you feel?" If he answers yes, continue with "Why don't we write the points down that you want to think about, so that if I cannot clarify them, I can give them to my manager and come back with the answers?"

If your prospective customer agrees to this, write the information down, confirm that what you have been told are the only reasons stopping him from moving forward, and then clarify the answers yourself or call your manager for assistance.

Your goal is to find out what your potential customer wants to think about, and this questioning technique will often put your customer in the position of telling you. He may even realize that there really isn't anything to think about, so he responds by confirming his commitment, which allows you the opportunity to assume the sale by asking for his signature to move forward.

### Example 3

"Mr. Jones, I understand you want to think about it. I feel that I am creating undue pressure, and that's the last thing I want to do. I only want to help you make what I believe would be the right decision. And I wouldn't be so persistent if I didn't really believe it would help you. Please let me know what I need to do in order to make this work for you."

Most people need time to think before they make a commitment to something, and the size of the sale will usually dictate how much thinking time they require.

Customize these examples to suit your personality and situation. Be authentic and portray a genuine interest in doing what is right for your customer, not yourself. Achieving customer commitment means taking all the basic ingredients and then molding them with your personality, sincerity and the belief that your product will really benefit your customer. Your response should follow the well-structured and comprehensive interaction you have had with your potential customer from the first meeting. After every customer interaction, analyze your results in order to improve future experiences.

Although there will be times when your customer genuinely wants to think about the decision, there will also be opportunities where she just needs more reassurance. Through their questioning, the sales pro recognizes the difference and, if time is needed to review the decision, provides written confirmation of the product differentiation, matching benefits, results the customer will receive and the return on investment. The sales pro will then ask for an appointment commitment to follow up and review the details, ensuring the date is within the time frame that allows the salesperson to still offer the incentives that have been presented.

This is the worst-case scenario and is not recommended until you have tried to first uncover what it is the customer really wants to think about. The problem with "I'll think about it" is that you have nothing to work with. They aren't giving you an objective reason that you can overcome or answer. Therefore, you have to find out what the objective reason is.

# CLOSING

## CARTOON STORY

BUT WHAT IF YOU'VE DONE EVERYTHING RIGHT AND THEY STILL SAY "I'll THINK IT OVER?"

THAT'S OBVIOUSLY GOING TO HAPPEN. WHEN IT DOES YOU'LL LEARN FROM OUR WORKBOOK WHAT TO SAY SO YOU CAN HANDLE IT.

REHEARSE? YOU MEAN LIKE REHEARSING YOUR PRESENTATION?

WELL, WHEN I KNOW WHAT TO SAY IN RESPONSE, WON'T THAT BE THE MAGIC INGREDIENT?

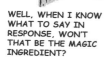

NO. AS I'VE ALREADY SAID, THERE ISN'T A MAGIC INGREDIENT. THE MOST IMPORTANT THING YOU CAN LEARN IS TO REHEARSE YOUR RESPONSES TO PROBLEMS LIKE "I WANT TO THINK ABOUT IT." THIS WILL HELP YOU CLOSE MORE SALES.

EXACTLY! EVERYONE IS SO EAGER TO LEARN THEIR PRESENTATION AND OF COURSE IT IS IMPORTANT. BUT TO REHEARSE AND LEARN TWO OR THREE RESPONSES TO EACH CLOSING SITUATION IS EQUALLY IMPORTANT.

YES, I SEE THAT NOW. IT GIVES YOU MORE CONFIDENCE TOO, BECAUSE YOU KNOW THAT AT THE END OF YOUR PRESENTATION, IF YOU GET AN OBJECTION, YOU'LL BE ABLE TO HANDLE IT OR ANSWER IT.

YES. THAT'S RIGHT. REMEMBER THOUGH, JUST LIKE YOUR PRESENTATION, YOU MUST FIRST LEARN THE CORRECT WAY BY THE BOOK. WHEN YOU CAN DO IT FROM MEMORY, MOLD YOUR PERSONALITY AROUND IT SO IT SOUNDS NATURAL.

WHAT IF THEY WANT TO RESEARCH THE COMPETITION?

THAT'S WHERE IT'S UP TO YOU TO HAVE MADE YOURSELF AWARE OF THE DIFFERENCE BETWEEN YOUR PRODUCT AND THE COMPETITOR'S.

## Business Pending

The subject of achieving final customer commitment would not be complete without discussing the time you spend on your business pending list or forecast. Sales pros balance their focus, time and energy on managing their existing accounts while finding and creating new opportunities. They never concentrate just on business they think might come in from previous presentations.

On the other hand, average sales people can fall into the trap of constantly spending their time calling on previous prospective customers who left them hanging with "I'll think about it," or "Send me a proposal." They hope that when they call again, the prospective customer is going to say, "Oh wow, thank goodness, I've been looking for your telephone number everywhere. I want to move forward." It rarely happens. Be creative while thinking of new ways to achieve final customer commitment from your business pending list, but don't allow this list to detract from your overall focus.

Creative ways to establish whether your business pending is real and to move opportunities forward include:

1.  Create a reason to present the system you are proposing if you haven't already.

2.  Offer the potential of a reduced cost. Tell your customer that although, as you understand it, price is not an issue, there is an opportunity to get an even better price. (Be creative and offer justification for the reduction.) Then ask if she would be interested. If so, tell her that you will find out what the new price would be and get straight back to her, preconfirming that due to inventory you would require an immediate decision. If she doesn't bite at this, there is a good chance she will mention a reason you were not previously aware of as to why she cannot take advantage of the special price, which gives you the opportunity to respond. Telling your customer you will get back to them with a price instead of just giving it to them on your initial call increases your credibility because your customer isn't feeling pressured to quickly make a decision, and the length of time between your initial call and when you call back creates the perception that this really

is a special deal that requires some kind of management approval. Confirming you will find out what the new price will be also allows them to respond, "Don't bother, I can't make the decision to move forward yet anyway," which offers you the opportunity to ask why or gain a better understanding of how interested they really are.

3.  Get your customer emotionally involved. People like to buy from people they like, so get creative. Explain that you are involved in a travel incentive or contest, and if her order were to come in this month, you would have the chance to win. Confirm that you hadn't mentioned it because you thought the sale was going to move forward earlier. Now that it's close to the end of the month or quarter, however, her order would really help you win. You'll be surprised at how many people want to help, and even if they can't, you'll likely get the real reason as to why they can't confirm the sale.

Always keep your authenticity, regardless of how creative you are. Your complete belief in your product and how it will benefit your customer is absolutely critical, especially when using an emotional connection to trigger the sale or establish the real reason for not moving forward. It's your job to do whatever it takes to continually move potential sales forward and reduce the amount of time hoping and waiting for the customer's call.

Try it for yourself: At the beginning of the month, make a list of pending business. At the end of the month, see how much business actually came in. When you review the list, you may be surprised at how little of the pending business you actually closed. Analyze how you can transition pending business into orders while you continue to focus on new business development. You will get more constructive work done, and you will find yourself placing new orders. At the same time, business that has been pending will come trickling in by itself. Always analyze what calls you are making, because if you are just focusing on pending business by constantly calling or writing to customers, you are confusing activity with accomplishment.

## When Striking Out

Although losing out on a potential sale is the last thing you want, the situation is bound to occur during your career. Learn from each situation and ask yourself questions regarding where you went wrong, how you can improve, and how you can benefit next time. Even after you make a sale, it's wise to analyze your experiences to gain a deeper understanding of why you achieved the sale or why you did not. This information helps you to grow as a professional salesperson and ultimately increases your chances of success in the future.

Ask yourself:

Did I ask for commitment too early?

Did I get too technical?

Did I match benefits properly?

Did I gather enough information?

Did I test the water to ascertain the customer's level of interest to move forward?

Did I build the importance of my matching benefits?

Did I get the customer emotionally involved?

Did I fail to answer a genuine objection?

Did I arrive already thinking the customer was not going to buy?

Did I give a reason to buy today?

Did I annoy my prospective customer with my mannerisms?

## Exercise

Think back to your current business pending list and write down two possible actions you could take to progress the sale.

### CUSTOMER #1

Reason for waiting? _____

Have you met with the decision maker? _____

Have you identified all the influencers? _____

Full presentation performed? _____

Incentive offered? _____

Options:

1) _____

2) _____

### CUSTOMER #2

Reason for waiting? _____

Have you met with the decision maker? _____

Have you identified all the influencers? _____

Full presentation performed? _____

Incentive offered? _____

Options:

1) _____

2) _____

# GOALS

CARTOON STORY

EXACTLY... IF I DON'T KNOW WHERE I'M GOING, HOW CAN I GET THERE?

OH, I SEE, YOU MEAN TO NOT HAVE A GOAL IS LIKE HAVING NO DESTINATION ON A MAP.

YES, WE JUST WANDER AND WANDER IN ALL DIRECTIONS, GETTING SWAYED BY WHATEVER DISTRACTS US.

SO WHAT HAPPENS IF YOU HAVE A DESTINATION?

WELL, LET'S SEE.... LOOK AT THE MAP AGAIN AND TELL ME WHERE JORDAN STREET IS.

MAP

O.K. JORDAN STREET. THERE IT IS.

GOOD, SO NOW YOU HAVE YOUR DESTINATION FOUND, WHICH COULD BE YOUR GOAL.

LIKE A NEW CAR STEREO SYSTEM OR EVEN A HOUSE!

ABSOLUTELY... HOWEVER, YOU SHOULD HAVE SHORT-TERM GOALS AND LONG-TERM ONES. THE SHORT-TERM ONES ARE LIKE STEPPING STONES THAT KEEP YOU MOTIVATED TOWARDS YOUR LONG-TERM ONE. NOW THAT YOU KNOW WHERE JORDAN STREET IS, TELL ME HOW TO GET THERE.

O.K., WRITE THIS DOWN... YOU GO ONTO THE A12 MOTORWAY, TO THE MALLARD DRIVE TURNOFF, TURN LEFT AT THE END OF THE SLIP ROAD, THEN RIGHT AT MALLARD DRIVE, LEFT AT THE END OF MALLARD TO PEACOCK ROAD... AT THE END OF PEACOCK TURN RIGHT ONTO HANSEN STREET - THE FIRST TURN ON YOUR LEFT WILL BE JORDAN STREET...

# CARTOON RECAP QUESTIONS

a) What would Pete's average order value be if he had achieved $35,000 in sales?

b) What is Pete's call to appointment ratio?

c) What is Pete's appointment to sale ratio?

- If Pete achieved $50,000 in sales, made sixty appointments out of the same number of calls and closed twelve sales, what would be his: a) call-to-appointment ratio? b) appointment-to-sale ratio? c) average order value?

## 7) PROSPECTING.................................................................... 85

- What companies does Pete recommend we focus on after we have been selling for a few months?
- What technique is John (Marie and Pete's friend) using to obtain appointments?
- How does Pete keep disciplined, and what objective does he establish each day?
- What formula do Pete and Marie discuss that confirms to them how much they are being paid for each new business call?
- Using the formula, how much would Pete be paid per call if the commission were 15%?
- What else has Pete learned that helps maintain his motivation to keep prospecting for new appointments?

## 8) PRE-PRESENTATION ................................................. 95

- What's the first thing Julie confirms when she arrives to present her product?
- What's the next stage she progresses to once she has established the decision makers are there?
- What's the third stage?
- What's the fourth stage?
- How long does it normally take for Julie to cover the pre-presentation process?
- What does poor selling create?

- How does Julie explain the difference between reducing your price to the ridiculous and difference pricing?
- Instead of the word *price*, what is Pete now going to use?
- What is Pete taught to do once he has quoted the price?
- What does Julie also add to help close the sale?
- What close is mentioned by Julie and Pete that is probably the most powerful and effective?

- What three words does Pete learn to help him respond to difficult objections?
- What does Julie do when she gets an easy objection?
- What process does Julie use when she gets an easy objection?
- When Julie gets a difficult objection, how does she confirm whether it's important to the customer or not?
- What is Pete taught to isolate?
- With a difficult objection, how would we first establish that the objection is valid?
- What process is Pete taught by Julie to help overcome a difficult objection?

- What magic ingredient does Pete find?
- What does Pete learn sells itself?
- What close does Julie mention that is probably the most powerful and convenient to use?
- What is Pete told to rehearse?
- Pete asks how to handle a response like "I want to research the competition." What advice is he given?

- What's the first thing Pete learns about goals?
- What two types of goal is Pete told he should have?
- What is Pete told he should do once he has a goal?
- What should Pete do to eliminate distractions?

# CARTOON
# RECAP
# ANSWERS

- To think about how you sound and look when you're talking about your personal belief. It helps to ensure that you are sounding and looking the same when you are talking about your product.
- Contact happy customers, remember when they first sold or reflect on how enthusiastic they were when they first started in sales.
- By comparing how he sounded when he was talking about his personal belief and his product.

- Selling the result of her product's benefits.
- A one-inch hole.

- It gives a better understanding of how your product will help and how it could help additional people or departments. It also adds more weight to your sale and makes it easier to justify.
- A closing opportunity.
- The order size could increase.

- It's a question that asks for more information regarding your previous question.
- Because it gives you more in-depth information.

- That your picture and solution are the same as theirs.
- Write down the answers and repeat back what the customer has said.

- The law of numbers.
- His results will improve and he will achieve more with the same number of calls.

- a) $5,833      b) 1 in 16      c) 1 in 6.
- a) 1 in 10      b) 1 in 5      c) $4,166.

- Focus on the industry or type of individuals you have sold to.
- Referral Prospecting.
- To keep consistent with new calls, always finish what you start and set an objective of so many calls or hours, and don't stop until you have reached that objective.
- Divide the total number of calls it takes to get a sale by your average commission for each sale.
- $9.37.
- When you do get an appointment, you are usually not competing against competition.

- Whether there is anyone else who needs to be present regarding the decision or usage of the product.
- A small introduction of her company and client list.
- Recap what had been discussed previously and reflect back the customer's current problem areas.
- Get a pre-commitment.
- 15 minutes.
- Objections.

- Ask as many questions as possible and incorporate the answers to his initial questions during the presentation, therefore burying the presentation.
- Remind the customer how that particular benefit will be of use compared to what she is presently doing.
- If he were to lead into his presentation just showing all that it could do and not relating it to the customer.
- The presentation becomes tailor-made to the customer.

- From the information she gathered during her initial questions.
- A benefit that matches the customer's need.
- The importance of the matching benefit gets diluted.

- Matching benefits.
- By getting the customer to talk about the identified problem.
- Get them to talk about it so they realize there could be a better way.
- Pre-commitment.

- Fear, Profit, Pride, Need, Love.
- Continue to push on the emotional reason for buying.
- No, it's one of many.
- Look around the customer's home or office; what you see could show you that they buy quality, keep things until they break or are very image conscious.
- Their current product is old and they are fearful of being without should it break.
- Ice-cold presentation.

- Reducing your price to the ridiculous is breaking down the price to a more justifiable figure. Difference pricing is only quoting the difference between what the customer is paying and what you are proposing they pay, or what the competition's price is and what yours is.
- Investment.
- Recap the matching benefits.
- A reason to buy today.
- Assume the sale.

- Feel, Felt, Found.
- Uses it to close the sale.
- Acknowledge what the customer said, isolate if necessary and then use it to close by saying, "If I could, would you …."
- Ask the customer why it's so important.
- The easy or difficult objection.
- Asking the customer to reconfirm why it is so important.
- Acknowledge it, rephrase it, ask why it is so important, confirm acceptance of their answer, isolate it, minimize the objection, maximize the matching benefits and re-close for the sale.

- None.
- A good presentation.
- The assumed close.
- Responses to problems/objections like "I want to think about it."
- Make yourself aware of the differences between your product and that of your competitors.

- Instead of going out today because that's what we did yesterday, go out with a specific purpose.
- Short-term goals and long-term ones.
- To set a plan or map of how to get it.
- Establish a time limit.

# THE FINAL WORD

The sales person who learns all there is to learn, who acts on that knowledge, who creates a goal to achieve and who is consistent in trying to achieve it will without doubt become successful. It can take time to get to the top and achieve true sales pro status, but as time passes, your foundation will be getting stronger and stronger.

Never give up on your sales goals. The rewards of a selling career will make the journey well worthwhile. If you take this profession to its fullest potential, you will discover there are no limits and you'll have ultimate power over your direction in life. Many sales people have tried to take the road toward becoming a professional salesperson but have fallen by the wayside or turned off the road for an easier but far less rewarding career. Their inability to finish the journey should be your motivation to keep traveling. You are responsible for your own successes and your own failures; never blame anyone else. You will succeed, as long as you make the calls.

There is only one limitation in life, and that is the one you put in your mind. You are what you believe. Whether you think you can or think you cannot, you're absolutely right. Remember, the only person who makes a mistake is the person who does nothing at all.

My hope is that you have adopted the information within this book and done all that is needed to become a professional salesperson. You're now ready to work toward attaining the tremendous results that selling can offer.

Good luck!

—Paul

# ABOUT THE AUTHOR

Paul Anderson's sales career started when he sold his way into a sales position for a Fortune 100 corporation, although he was two years below the company's minimum age requirement. He immediately hit the ground running, achieving Sales Rookie of the Year, and continued to break all previous sales records, earning over twenty sales awards, a nomination for worldwide salesperson of the year and a seat on the prestigious sales advisory board. He was also elected a member of the order of sales excellence earning the title "Machine, Not a Man"—all by the age of 25.

The selling skills and techniques that he uses and teaches every day have earned him the top sales position with multiple companies that sell products and services in the business-to-business and business-to-consumer markets, and with sales cycles that are both long and short.

Paul has accumulated 25-plus years of top sales and leadership achievement. His passion for the world of selling is shown through the remarkable results he consistently achieves both in sales and sales leadership and through his sales mentor program where he remains committed to helping people without sales experience get into sales and immediately earn an income they hadn't thought possible. Paul resides in San Diego, California, with his wife and three children.